Handbook of Church Correspondence

By G. CURTIS JONES

Repairing Our Religion

On Being Your Best

Which Way Is Progress?

What Are You Worth?

In Their Light We Walk

What Are You Doing?

Youth Deserves to Know

March of the Year

Parents Deserve to Know

Handbook of Church Correspondence

Handbook of
Church
Correspondence

G. CURTIS JONES

The Macmillan Company NEW YORK

A DIVISION OF THE CROWELL-COLLIER PUBLISHING COMPANY

MACMILLAN NEW YORK, LONDON

First Printing

The Macmillan Company, New York
Brett-Macmillan Ltd., Galt, Ontario
Macmillan New York, London

Printed in the United States of America

Library of Congress catalog card number: 62-15689

To Becky and Curtis

Contents

Introduction

Have you ever lived for a letter? Day after day you waited and there was no mail. Someone has to write for you to receive a letter. And you have to write for another to be satisfied.

After several long, lonesome days in Africa, one afternoon I received twelve letters, and all but one were handwritten! What a surprise! What a joy! Immediately I was refreshed in body, mind, and spirit.

Letter writing is the distinctive and personal art of communicating information, greetings, commitments, and love. Nothing in all literature is more sacred, profound, and permanent than a well motivated and expressed letter.

Like all responsible assignments requiring artistic skill and sensitivity, letter writing is always in danger of disappearing as an art. This does not imply that automation and mass communications are outmoding the postal system. Quite the opposite is true. Our complex technological society has greatly increased the flow of mail. The average American receives and sends about three hundred fifty pieces of mail a year. It is estimated that within the next twenty-five years the amount will double. Witness the unprecedented building boom in post offices and expansion in postal services.

Though all citizens are receiving and sending more mail than ever before—the bulk of which is routine and volume-produced—imagination and personal charm are all too seldom found among our pyramids of communications. Cold and careless letter writing is so common that many corporations and business firms are not only employing counselors in correspondence but are even sponsoring letter-writing clinics. Some commercial houses periodically award prizes to the writers of the best letters in their various departments. A resurgence of interest in good letter writing is apparent.

More than one hundred fifty individuals, representing a wide geographical spread and vocational involvement, were invited to contribute to this book. I was amazed at the number of so-called "prominent" people who admitted they were poor letter writers and therefore had nothing to contribute. Many submitted letters, apologizing for them, but willing to be "exposed" for the sake of gaining assistance in this much neglected area of public relations and personal communication.

It should also be said that the author has been in correspondence with all the living contributors. Letters discreetly included to illustrate certain points are not to be lauded more appreciatively or criticized more severely than any honest writer would censor his own effort. Wherever advisable the authors of letters are cited, otherwise they appear anonymously. By their very nature some communications could not be identified; others in the category of anonymity were furnished by the author. In all instances, whether indicated or not, permission to use material was secured. As a result of this cooperation, this volume is generously sprinkled with exceptional and masterful letters from the past and present.

I am grateful to the Post Office Department for its permission to use an unusual amount of helpful information, as well as to a host of splendid correspondents across the country.

It is hoped that HANDBOOK OF CHURCH CORRESPONDENCE will stimulate additional interest in good correspondence. While the greater part of the book is cast in the context of the church, its methods, philosophy, skill, and spirit are applicable to all professions and vocations.

I acknowledge the assistance of all those who stimulated my thinking in this area, especially Mr. Marvin G. Osborn, Washington University, St. Louis, Missouri; Dr. Lionel A. Whiston, Jr., Eden Theological Seminary, Webster Groves, Missouri, for their counsel

and editorial assistance; and my family and church colleagues for
living with me through the inception and delivery of another book.
Genuine gratitude is expressed to my secretary, Ruth Lloyd Bethge,
for research and preparation of the manuscript. Without her me-
thodical perseverance the book could not have been produced on
schedule.

G. CURTIS JONES

Johannesburg
September, 1961

Handbook of Church Correspondence

1

"Has the Mail Come?"

There is an indescribable eagerness and ecstasy about receiving mail. Regardless of weather or terrain, soldiers will quickly and gladly assemble for mail call. Between classes, campus students rush to the post office, hoping for a message from home, fiancée, friends, or just anybody. Elderly people silently and patiently await the arrival of their common priest the postman, praying he will brighten their day with a card or letter from his leather pouch of surprises. Citizens of small communities queue at the single window of the village post office and plaintively ask, "Any mail for us today?"

Like picking up a hand of cards in a bridge game, the opening of letters is filled with suspense and surprise. Unlike card playing, however, the elements of chance and distribution are virtually nil. One's mail is the result of specific action. A personal letter is unique. It is the private commerce of mind and heart directed to a single person for a particular reason. John Donne, sixteenth century English poet-preacher, once wrote to Sir Henry Wotton,

> More than kisses, letters mingle souls;
> For, thus friends absent speak.

1

THE SIGNIFICANCE OF IT ALL

The United States Postal Service is the greatest communications system on earth. It is the lifeblood of our commercial life; the handmaiden of our free press; the fabric that binds our social life together.

Uncensored, efficient, serving 175 million of our citizens daily, the United States Post Office Department is a basic life force that gives practical meaning to our free way of life.

Without an efficient modern postal service our nation would be seriously weakened.[1]

The free, uncensored Postal Service of the United States is the greatest communication system in history. It is the arm of our government which serves more of our people more directly than any other. It has helped to build our great industries; it has helped weld our people into a great nation, and it is today one of the bulwarks of our national strength in maintaining our progress and preserving our freedom.[2]

UNITED STATES POSTAL SERVICE

Americans send and receive two-thirds of all the mail in the world. There are approximately 36,000 post offices in the United States with 89,399 delivery routes in the cities of the nation. According to the Post Office Department, Washington, in 1959 there were 61,247 million pieces of originating mail posted in America. This represents 882.9 million cubic feet of originating mail and 11,332 million pounds. The number of pieces of mail per citizen per year now approaches 350 and is expected to double within twenty-five years.

Automation has invaded the postal system. Mechanized equipment is rapidly breaking up the old bottlenecks, and modern electrical systems have literally energized the postal department. Think of a facing and canceling machine (first-class letters) processing

[1] Arthur E. Summerfield, Postmaster General of the United States, 1953–1961.
[2] J. Edward Day, Postmaster General of the United States. Letter dated June 19, 1961. Used by permission.

thirty thousand pieces an hour! Giant "cullers" quickly separate letters from other mail.

In the year 1850 it required about twenty-four days to transport a letter from coast to coast; today, about five hours. Moreover, with the aid of photoelectric eyes, sending and receiving equipment, important letters will be flashed instantaneously and invisibly across our land. Communications are a vital part of an indispensable link in a country's economy and development. The postal service is a main artery in the circulatory system of a nation's health.

The vast flow of mail across our country is the multiplication of personal correspondence. Have you ever visualized your letter in this mountain of mail?

STATIONERY

The appeal of a letter may be greatly enhanced by the appropriateness of the stationery. A church office should have more than one size and style of letterhead. The usual standard page, 8½ x 11 inches, is acceptable for most purposes, yet it seems much too large and formal for the more intimate letters of the pastor. Moreover, taste varies with churches and ministers as to the composition of the letterhead. Church stationery can be gaudy and cluttered with names, titles, pictures, and mottoes. More often than not a good-quality white paper is much preferred to pastels and brilliant colors. The quiet dignity and texture of the paper communicates its own message.

MIMEOGRAPHED AND PERSONAL LETTERS

Methods of duplicating letters range from the old jerky, inky, manually operated mimeographing machine to high-speed photo and offset printing. Large mailings necessitate duplicated letters. Care should be exercised to ascertain quality work and attractiveness. A church with a sizable membership needs a good workroom where its mailings are produced and processed. The counsel of public relations, advertising, and efficiency experts proves valuable in determining the kind of equipment best suited for the need.

It may be more economical and practical at times to engage the services of a good letter-writing concern. However and whenever the duplicated letter is used, it should meet all requirements of good correspondence. Effort should be made to make the mimeographed letter warm and friendly, and, whenever possible, it should be personally signed. A familiar signature tends to personalize and dignify an otherwise stereotyped message. There is a definite place for the duplicated letter, though one should realize its limitations and never employ it to accomplish a really first-class job. Very few souls are won through this medium, and not many budgets are balanced.

A personal letter differs from a duplicated one in that it is directed to a particular person for a specific reason. The salutation is formal or informal as the occasion demands. It may be typed or it may be handwritten. The personal letter—the intimate commerce between minds and hearts—is among the most beautiful, sacred, and profound of literary attainments. One is at his best, or should be, in personal correspondence. Photographically speaking, a letter is the glossy print of the sender. It is inseparably associated with the author and reflects his personality, idiosyncrasies, and genuineness. A personal letter should always be sealed and bear first-class postage.

The postscript is usually considered an afterthought written at the bottom of the page and designated by "P.S." However, it may well be the most important sentence or sentences of the letter. It is frequently employed for emphasis. The author may assert himself or apologize in the postscript.

Writers of personal letters should strive for the perfection attributed to Bernard Shaw by his admirer and friend Mrs. Patrick Campbell, who said, "If I could write letters like you, I would write letters to God."

CARBONS AND FILING

There should be copies of all church correspondence, whether handwritten, typed, or mimeographed. If the letter is typed, high-quality carbon paper should be used and as many legible copies made as desirable. Every letter and reply should be dated, stapled, and filed. If the sender does not wish to have his initials appear on the original, then a notation should go on the carbon to identify writer and transcriber.

Filing is a science in itself. It can be very complicated. Some filing systems are so involved that it requires a system to keep the system! These simple suggestions may be helpful in church filing.

1. *Alphabetical Files.* All systems of filing should start with an alphabetical file. From this they may fan out into categories, itemized departments, reference and idea classifications.

2. *Current Files.* All written materials issued from a church— letters, bulletins, papers—should be filed when they appear and kept for at least a year or until the expiration of the statute of limitations. Bulletins and periodicals should be filed annually for reference and record.

3. *Perpetual Files.* In this category are carry-over materials, the usefulness of which occurs periodically.

4. *Inactive Files.* This is the material from current files of a previous period; some files are transferred annually, other material is retained in the active files for as long as three years. The end of the church year is a logical time to reevaluate, reclassify, and transfer files.

5. *Categorized Files.* Itemized files, such as these, set out the responsibilities and related connections of the minister and staff. For instance, within the scope of *Administration* would fall staff, departmental reports of the official board and minutes of important congregational meetings. One would file responsibilities to related and unrelated groups under *Associations and Organizations. Business* would contain copies of *Budget, Financial Reports, Fund Raising,* and all matters pertaining to finance.

6. *Personal Files.* Every pastor or church administrator needs a confidential file at his fingertips. Intimate correspondence should be filed in this section, preferably in a locked file or desk.

7. *Sermon and Idea File.* Every preacher struggles with the problem of filing his sermons, that is, if he writes them! The more commonly used index systems are the (*a*) Topical, (*b*) Textual, (*c*) Seasonal (Special Days), (*d*) Yearly, and (*e*) Monthly.

This would apply also to a file for *Prayers.*

An *idea* file is of invaluable assistance to the minister, who from time to time clips material which will be of use to him in his work. Many ministers, in addition to the duties of their pastorates, speak publicly for various organizations and meetings. Timely topics can be quickly reviewed when filed for ready reference.

8. *Follow-up File.* This is the working file, responsibility for which falls directly on the minister's secretary or assistant. Correspondence which relates to forthcoming events and responsibilities are classified in this "don't-let-me-forget" file. One efficacious system is set with the months of the year, the numerical dates following, and as the days go on, as well as the months, material comes automatically to hand. For instance, December has behind it all the days of the month, 1 through 31. A meeting has been set for the 10th, the notices mailed on the 2nd. The morning of the 10th, markup is pulled from pending matters of the 10th and given to the minister or administrator.

Finally, if files are set in proper order, an index should be typed with copies for those interested in or responsible for the material in the entire system. Such a list can save time when correspondence is needed quickly.

WHAT'S LEFT IN YOUR FILES?

When a minister is transferred or called to another parish, inevitably his work is evaluated. There are those who take very seriously facility improvements, the number of people added to the membership, and the status of the budget. Indeed there are many ways to appraise a man's ministry. However, we sometimes forget church files and records. What tangible continuity has the minister left for his successor? The minister's files speak volumes. What do you have in your files?

Things to Avoid

Church correspondence, like everything that emanates from the House of the Lord, should excel. While unattractive and unbecoming letters may represent some institutions without hurting their reputation, not so with the church. Carelessness and inaccuracies are not to be associated with perfection, the standard of the Christian. Therefore those who are privileged to correspond for the church should attempt to avoid:

1. *Ambiguity.* A good letter should be clear, convincing, and

complete. To answer a letter by saying, "The matter referred to in yours of the seventeenth is before me and, strangely enough, I find myself in total agreement," does not say anything to anyone except the principals involved, and perhaps not too much to them. There is little advantage in filing the carbon of such a letter.

2. *Abruptness.* Words can be hard and cruel, especially in print when they are detached from the personality of the writer.

3. *Carelessness.* The majority of our mistakes are caused by carelessness. Review your letter, revamp it if necessary, make it an impeccable representative of you and your church.

4. *Inaccurate spelling and use of words.* Incorrect spelling and inaccurate use of words are annoying. The church office, indeed every desk, should be equipped with a good dictionary and a thesaurus.

5. *Erasures.* A good correspondent will avoid sending a letter containing corrections and erasures. An alert minister will not permit poorly produced mail to go out over his signature from the church he serves.

6. *Excessive length.* A good letter can be too long! Generally speaking—there are exceptions—a letter that will not fit on a standard page is too long. It does not require a professional writer to detect sentences and paragraphs that should be shortened or deleted. However, should the nature of the matter at hand require more than a single page, succeeding pages should be of similar size, color, and quality paper, without letterhead markings, that is, plain paper. The addressee's name should appear in the upper left-hand corner (William R. Brown, continued), the number of the page in the top center, and the date harmonizing with the right-hand margin, depending, of course, upon preferred format. The point is to make certain that all pages following the initial page are clearly identified with the salutation.

7. *Excessive brevity.* Though most of us need to work for brevity, a letter can be so brief that it leaves the impression that the writer missed the point, that the answer is too unimportant and the sender too busy to be human. A sentence or two of warmth and gratitude are always appreciated, though the letter could be answered "Yes" or "No."

8. *Poor equipment.* It is most difficult, if not impossible, to produce an attractive letter with poor equipment.

9. *Dogmatism.* Karl Barth once declared that if there is one thing

the Christian cannot be dogmatic about, it is dogmatics. This is true also of church correspondence. Confidence is commendable, but overconfidence is irritating.

WHAT CONSTITUTES A GOOD LETTER?

A letter is personality expressed on paper. It is an individual speaking from a page, communicating his thoughts, wishes, and concerns. A letter is much more than a handwritten note or the typescript of a technical document properly addressed, stamped, and mailed. It is a personal ambassador, a versatile and dependable representative. Many times a letter is routine and inconsequential. On other occasions it is a persuasive salesman knocking at the door of a prospective customer miles away. Frequently the letter is the voice of comfort and love communicating the deepest emotions of the human heart.

1. *A good letter will be attractive.* Its general appearance usually will determine the consideration it will receive.

2. *A good letter will be a thoughtful communication.* The sender will endeavor to evaluate the situation that initiated the correspondence, plan his approach, carefully select and weigh his words, write a rough draft and walk around it for size and sense.

3. *A good letter will stimulate the imagination.* The writer of a personal message, like the author of a book, must not only be able to visualize the reader's reaction, but he must also arouse within the reader the ability to see his point of view and to share his enthusiasm.

4. *A good letter will demand attention.* It is difficult to ignore a letter which is carefully planned, psychologically timed, and succinctly phrased.

5. *A good letter will excite interest.* Whether its purpose is to console the bereaved or to sell a bill of goods, the communication must breathe genuine interest and understanding.

6. *A good letter will establish confidence.* A proper rapport is imperative for any important transmission of ideas.

7. *A good letter will convey cooperation.* Whenever possible, it will discreetly offer alternative courses of action.

8. *A good letter will reflect character.* Not only a person's speech but also his written words will identify him.

9. *A good letter will communicate intent.* During the agitated days before the Civil War, when Southern leaders did not trust Lincoln and his Northern friends were urging him to write something specific regarding slavery, he replied with this masterful letter.

SPRINGFIELD, ILLINOIS
October 23, 1860

MY DEAR SIR:

Yours of the 13th was duly received. I appreciate your motive when you suggest the propriety of my writing for the public something disclaiming all intention to interfere with slaves or slavery in the states; but in my judgment it would do no good. I have already done this many, many times; and it is in print, and open to all who will read. Those who will not read or heed what I have already publicly said would not read or heed a repetition of it. "If they hear not Moses and the prophets, neither will they be persuaded though one rose from the dead."

Yours truly,
A. LINCOLN [3]

PROMPTNESS AND POLITENESS

Everyone likes to receive letters, yet it is astonishing how little mail some people receive! This would be expected of recluses and "characters," but one is surprised to discover that otherwise well regulated families seldom write one another. When I asked a boy in a splendid eastern university about his parents, he replied: "I don't know. They never write to me." The tone of voice communicated disappointment and wistfulness.

Whatever the nature of the correspondence, it demands promptness and politeness. The integrity and ethics of letter writing are as demanding as those which compel one to answer the door if he is home, the telephone when it rings, or to speak when addressed. To permit one's mail to accumulate is inexcusable and suggests indecision.

[3] Charles W. Moore (ed.), *Lincoln—Addresses and Letters* (New York: American Book Company, 1914), p. 137. Used by permission.

Many busy people agree the time to answer mail is when it comes. While the mood of receiving it is still present, that is the time to reply. There are letters, of course, which require soul-searching, research, and consultation with colleagues and associates before they can be answered. Even so, these can be promptly acknowledged, advising the sender of difficulties involved, if any, and alerting him as to when he might expect a complete reply. The efficiency with which correspondence is handled makes an important impression. It indicates not only courtesy but also character.

There are many mechanical aids to expedite the handling of mail. Less formal people sometimes place two letter boxes on their desks, one marked "Incoming" and the other "Outgoing." Others identify their correspondence by the simple words "Today" and "Tomorrow," which usually means that mail received today should be answered no later than tomorrow. Some busy men develop a system of "follow-ups" and reminders, which quietly needle them into action. Others prefer that secretaries handle their mail almost entirely once a given pattern has been established. Irrespective of the office, the quantity of correspondence, or the gadgets employed, ultimately decisions must be made. Letters must be written. Though a letter may require revamping and reviewing by other departments within a corporation or church, to procrastinate is to minimize the cause and the sender.

However satisfactory a given system, there will be oversights and at times mistakes. Punctuality has its penalties, including tendencies toward impulsiveness, explosiveness, and inaccuracies. There are many ways by which the temptations of haste may be averted. It may help to use two letters, the first being a simple, brief acknowledgment. This provides a "cooling-off" period, if necessary, as well as time to develop a thoughtful and accurate answer. A second method of preventing the kind of replies which might distort truth and destroy friendship is to "share" a difficult letter. Your letter may sound entirely different when your secretary reads it back or when a member of your family or firm asks the implication of certain phrases.

While writing this chapter I received a letter from a friend who said she had found my unanswered letter in a file. Her six-page, beautifully phrased, handwritten letter was in effect an apology. This ardent baseball fan and follower of the St. Louis Cardinals had invited me to join a party at Busch Stadium on a given Sunday afternoon. Aside from the matter of conscience, it is a good thing I did not go, for we probably would have missed each other at the park, since she was six years answering my letter!

This wonderful person wrote:

> I simply want to express my appreciation for a man who has convictions and stands by them, and at the same time tell you how ashamed I am of my own lack of witness on those numerous weekends in St. Louis. . . . Anyway, thank you for what you said—even though it took over six years for it to sink in.

One would delight in receiving such a letter, however tardy, since it is the epitome of graciousness and genuineness.

WHEN TO WRITE

As in everything, the timing of a letter is extremely important. A premature message may be as annoying as a belated letter. If one is prompt in answering mail, he will have little difficulty in knowing when to reply. However, it is sometimes more difficult to determine when to initiate a letter.

There should be a definite reason for writing. Quite aside from the intricate and intriguing public relations techniques employed by corporations and institutions, individuals should also develop a calendar of responsibility, a listing of people who demand their attention, as well as those not yet numbered among their circle of clients and friends. It may be an anniversary, a request for information, a sales pitch, a problem, a need, a personal tragedy, a crisis. Whatever the nature of the communication, its timing should reveal alertness and thoughtfulness.

A letter is a link between two lives. At times the message comes only with labored effort. Sometimes the muse never comes, and again it is as effortless as breathing. Emerson knew this when he said, "In writing a letter to a friend, we may find that we rise to thought and to a cordial power of expression that costs no effort."

One will usually know when to write. His heart will haunt him. The real question is: Will he write when he knows he should?

RESPONSIBLE CORRESPONDENT

Religion, ethics, courtesy all combine to demand that we be responsible correspondents. A letter is a sealed secret, aching ambition, soulful sharing, one's mind and heart in black and white, and thus should be respected and protected. It is distressing to learn how some important people are insensitive in the handling of their correspondence. Whether they call it discretion or intelligent postponement, it has repercussions and lasting effects. I shall never forget writing a prominent pulpiteer about a matter of great concern to me. My impatience intensified with each passing week. His reply never came! After this experience, I must confess that my estimate of the man diminished.

Not long ago the chairman of a national church committee came to me with this concern. Among other things, she was responsible for developing and submitting a slate of officers at their annual meeting. She had written certain committeemen who had not replied. Indeed she had written some of them twice. When time had run out and selections had been made, the tardy committee members replied. Embarrassing changes had to be made.

We are responsible not only for *what* we write but also *when* we write!

LETTERS LIVE

Though ours is the day of increased population and income, television saturation, throughways, jet travel, and long-distance telephone calls, the letter still lives as a clear and comprehensive communication. Though the art of letter writing is disappearing all too rapidly, it is nevertheless used for every conceivable purpose and is accepted as final authority in negotiations and commitments. After the conversation is over, the sale completed, the appointment made, we usually say, "Will you drop me a line of confirmation?" or "I will send you a confirming letter tomorrow."

Letters are living documents. They are invaluable and permanent records. They are heralds! The written word is difficult to deny. Therefore we are at our best in correspondence when our motives are discernible and our undeniable selves are revealed.

2

Composition and Construction

REV. JONE'S:

I know you will be surprise to get A Letter from me. How's your Family getting along? Fine I hope. How are the Boy's getting along. I am asking you all For a little Money I am a Captain for my side. & I am asked to raise $300. for the use of our Basement. Our ending for this Drive will be The 4th Sun in Nov. So if you all can I will Thank you very much. May God Bless you.

Thank you

A. M.

Like most people, this person wrote the way she talked, indulging in ambiguous colloquialisms.

Nowhere is uninhibited self-expression so free and natural as in the personal letter. If one is careless in written communications, the chances are he will be inaccurate and unconvincing in his speech. If the message cannot be written, it cannot be spoken.

Since a letter is the most permanent and reliable of all emissaries, it is important that the writer be acquainted with some common rules of construction. More often than not, the letter is the first encounter with a stranger. It is therefore important that the introduction be correct, clear, and convincing.

13

THE SALUTATION

The introductory phrase of a letter is called the *salutation*. A correspondent must guard against being too formal, perfunctory, or presumptuous. Moreover, he must avoid the frigidity that accompanies such common greetings as "Dear Sir." There is a place, of course, for such formality, but rarely does it generate the warmth and interest of "Dear Mr. Brown," or "My dear Mr. Smith." (When not used as the first word in the salutation, "dear" is always spelled with a small *d*.) A less severe but still formal greeting would be "Dear Robert Brown," (not commonly used but correct).

Care should be exercised lest the addressee's name be incorrectly spelled or used. Most people are proud of their names and appreciate correctness. The writer should be sufficiently familiar with the person to whom he is writing to visualize him and to address him appropriately.

The problem of proper salutation inevitably introduces the complicated question of titles. Service personnel, government employees, and professional groups are particularly sensitive about protocol. It is a matter of social recognition and courtesy. Awkwardness in this area may result in embarrassment and denial.

FORM OF ADDRESS	SALUTATION
President of the United States Mr. John Fitzgerald Kennedy The White House Washington, D.C.	Dear Mr. President:
Governor The Honorable John M. Dalton Executive Mansion Jefferson City, Missouri	Dear Sir: Less formal and more intimate, Dear Governor Dalton:
Senator The Honorable Stuart Symington United States Senate Washington, D.C.	My dear Senator: Less formal, Dear Mr. Symington:

Congressman
  The Honorable Thomas B. Curtis   Dear Sir:
  United States House of Repre-   Less formal, Dear Mr. Curtis:
    sentatives
  Washington, D.C.

Mayor
  The Honorable Raymond R.   Dear Sir:
    Tucker   Less formal, Dear Mr. Mayor:
  Mayor's Office
  St. Louis, Missouri

Judge
  The Honorable Randolph H.   Dear Sir:
    Weber   Less formal, Dear Judge Weber:
  Federal Courts Building
  St. Louis, Missouri

University Chancellor
  Chancellor McGruder E. Sadler   Dear Chancellor Sadler:
  Texas Christian University   Less formal, Dear Dr. Sadler:
  Fort Worth, Texas

Pope
  His Holiness Pope John XXIII   Your Holiness:
  The Vatican
  Vatican City, Italy

Cardinal
  His Eminence Joseph Cardinal   Your Eminence:
    Ritter
  4396 Lindell Boulevard
  St. Louis, Missouri

Catholic Bishop
  The Most Reverend Glennon P.   Your Excellency:
    Flavin
  7148 Forsyth Boulevard
  St. Louis 5, Missouri

Catholic Priest
> The Reverend Joseph Cummins
> 428 Linn Street
> Brooktown, Missouri

Dear Sir:
Less formal, My dear Father Cummins:

Anglican Bishop
> The Right Reverend Robert R.
>   Brown, D.D.
> Episcopal Bishop of Arkansas
> Little Rock, Arkansas

Dear Bishop Brown:
Less formal greeting is reserved for family and intimate friends.

Methodist Bishop
> Bishop Gerald Kennedy
> Hollywood, California

Dear Bishop Kennedy:

Dean of a Cathedral
> The Very Reverend Ned Cole,
>   D.D.
> Christ Church Cathedral
> Thirteenth and Locust
> St. Louis 1, Missouri

Dear Dean Cole:
Or if the name is not used, Very Reverend Sir:

Dean of College, University or
Graduate School
> Dr. Liston Pope, Dean
> Yale Divinity School
> Yale University
> 409 Prospect Street
> New Haven, Connecticut

Dear Dean Pope:

Chaplain
> Lt. Col. Ernest E. Northen, Jr.
> Post and Division Chaplain
> Hdqrs, 101st A.B. Division
> Camp Breckinridge, Kentucky

Dear Chaplain Northen:
Irrespective of rank

Rabbi
> Rabbi Ferdinand M. Isserman
> 5017 Washington Avenue
> St. Louis 8, Missouri

Dear Rabbi Isserman:
Or, My dear Rabbi Isserman

President of a Business Firm
Dr. Wilbur H. Cramblet, President
Christian Board of Publication
Beaumont and Pine Streets
St. Louis 3, Missouri

Dear Dr. Cramblet:
[He has a Ph.D.] or, My dear Dr. Cramblet:

High School Principal
Dr. Mark Boyer
University City High School
6701 Delmar Boulevard
St. Louis 30, Missouri

Dear Dr. Boyer:

Athletic Coach
Mr. Jordan Olivar
Head Football Coach
Yale University
New Haven, Connecticut

Dear Mr. Olivar:
Or, Dear Coach Olivar: or, less formal, Dear Coach:

Minister
The Reverend William Coles Blackwell
First Christian Church
25 Trinity Place
Fort Thomas, Kentucky

My dear Mr. Blackwell:
If he has a doctorate, My dear Dr. Blackwell: *never* Dear Reverend:

College Student
Mr. John Vencill
Massachusetts Institute of Technology
Cambridge, Massachusetts

Dear Mr. Vencill:
Or less formal, Dear John: An adult writing to a college student would normally address him by his or her first name.

Corporation
General Motors Corporation
Detroit 2, Michigan

Gentlemen:
"Dear Sirs" is archaic and obsolete. Even in a general salutation when writing a corporation or an institution, it is desirable to address the communication to a particular person or to the head

of a department wherein your
complaint or request would logi-
cally fall.

Common Form
  Mr. Joseph F. Johnston   Dear Mr. Johnston:
  R.F.D. #3
  Appomattox, Virginia

THE BODY

A professor of journalism in Scotland used to say to his students,
after they handed in their essays, "Did it ever occur to you to tear
up the first page?" Knowing how difficult it is to begin any piece of
writing, the critical teacher operated on the theory that the first
page was usually superficial and pedantic. This is equally true of
correspondence. The first sentence, like an I-beam in a bridge, must
carry the traffic of the letter. It not only establishes tone but also
determines tonnage! The opening statement must be strong, clear,
and compelling.

Poor Beginnings

Dear Dr. Jones:
  I am writing to you to find out if my letter requesting . . .
was received by you. There was some mixup . . . and I just
wondered if it had been received or not.

The opening statement is repetitious and redundant.

Dear G. Curtis:
  It was awful good to hear from you again and to learn that
you are getting along good.

A paucity of skill!

Dear Brother Jones:
  This is the last letter which I will send this calendar year . . .

The instantaneous reaction to such a beginning is "Praise the
Lord!"

DEAR FRIEND:
   Will you kindly consider this letter as though written and personally signed? Numbers make printing necessary.

A weakness of the form letter is that it rarely fits the reader. It is stilted and cold. The word "numbers" is ambiguously and carelessly employed.

MY DEAR BROTHER JONES:
   It is good of you to send me *this note* under date of December 14 even if you must report a very disagreeable gathering.

Here is a case of an executive not reading back his mail or not thinking clearly at the time it was dictated. "This note" really refers to *my* letter to him.

DEAR CHRISTIAN FRIENDS:
   Please allow me to take this means of expressing to each and all of you my sincere appreciation for the fine spirit of cooperation manifest by you in promoting our recent successful fellowship meeting held in the interests of building a finer community spirit.

Although this is a sincere utterance, still the opening phrase "Please allow me" is a cliché and means little. The sentence is much too gushing and sweet, and the word "manifest" is used in the wrong tense.

Good Beginnings

DEAR REV. JONES:
   Thank you for your telegram with reference to the welfare of the teachers of _____. As I repeatedly pledged during the campaign and reiterated in my inaugural address, I am doing everything I can for the school teachers of _____ with the aid of the General Assembly.

Aside from the incorrect salutation, this is an excellent beginning. The term "Reverend" should never be used without the article "the" nor without being followed by "Mr." or "Dr." However, the paragraph contains good sentence structure and shows the writer's familiarity with the problems at hand. It is warm and friendly, yet comes directly to the point.

DEAR DR. JONES:

I just cannot resist the temptation to drop you a note and let you know "how right" you are in your analysis of Dr. _____.

My attention was immediately arrested by this opening sentence.

MY DEAR MR. JONES:

I appreciate very much your letter of the 6th, in which you express your views on compulsory military training. The sentence in your letter, "In view of the fact that our world is in such a turmoil that it seems unwise to establish policies now which may not at all coincide with the needs of the anticipated new world," impresses me very much. There are many things being proposed here at the present, and in my opinion the above quotation applies to them.

I will carefully consider and approach the matter of military training, and at the time it is considered on the floor of the House, I will bear in mind the views you have expressed.

A very succinct statement, followed by a clear declaration of intent.

DEAR JESSE:

Your letter of September 11 relative to the possibility of working in an Armed Forces Preaching Mission, was awaiting me upon my return to the office September 29 from a world trip.

Insofar as I can see my schedule, I would be able to help you the third week of January or the first two weeks of February. If it materializes, brother, please send me to a warm country!

This is a brief note to a close friend, containing the elements of positiveness coupled with humor.

DEAR DR. JONES:

Mr. _____, a sophomore in the College of Arts & Science here at the University, has applied for a student loan to help with his college expenses and has given us your name as a reference.

This paragraph comes directly to the point without wasted verbiage.

STRIKING LETTERS

Here are a few specimens of good correspondence. You will note the wide diversity in format, style, and tone.

July 1, 1951

MY DEAR CURTIS:

Thank you very much for taking time to write me, and so generously.

Gratefully yours,

January 30, 1956

DEAR DR. JONES:

Thank you for your letter of January 20 telling me that Dr. _____ of St. Louis and Mr. _____ of Nashville, Tennessee, are planning to be in Jerusalem about April 10.

I have already given their names to our office and you will hear from my son, Major _____, in this matter. I assure you I will do everything I can to make their visit interesting and profitable. It will be a pleasure to meet them.

Everything is so quiet now in Jordan and we hope it will continue to be so.

With my love to Sybil and the boys, I am

Yours sincerely,

January 5, 1960

DEAR CURTIS:

As I approached my desk this morning I could think of no better way to start the new year than to take a few minutes to express my appreciation for your opening sermon of the new year.

It was especially appropriate and stimulating. I am sure it touched many responsive chords.

Sincerely yours,

DEAR CURTIS:

I told you on Sunday that I was really helped by the service and especially by your sermon. Your quotation from Dan Poling,

"To journey is better than to arrive," brought to mind a phrase that we will be hearing and many thousand people will be reading this year. It is the statement that was carved above the entrance to the stadium in Los Angeles at the Olympic Games in 1932, "The glory is not in the winning but in striving well."

Sincerely yours,

A "NOTHING" LETTER

There is such a thing as being so precise and adroit that nothing is communicated or accomplished. There are times, of course, to exercise constraint and discretion, but to overindulge in these prerogatives is to deny the recipient of the letter what he wants—a clear answer.

This letter, from a high government official, illustrates my point.

DEAR DR. JONES:

Thank you for your favor of July eighth relative to the seven men from _____ who have been sentenced to the electric chair. I am glad to have this expression of your views, and I am sure you understand that my only desire is to do that which may be right and just in connection with this matter.

Very truly yours,

STYLE AND APPEARANCE

There is no inflexible rule regulating the exact style of a given letter, though circumstances demand a certain general format. One would not reply to an RSVP invitation with tablet and pencil, neither would he type a thank-you note for a wedding gift, nor convey condolences in a stiffly phrased dictated letter. There is a definite place for the intimate handwritten note. Like the grace of good manners, good style is never ostentatious. It is the natural synthesis of mind and heart seeking articulation.

Quite aside from correctness and appearance, style in writing is the distinctive "you" expressing an idea or conviction attractively and persuasively. Style is effective communication, personality, taste. Style is the unlabored consequence of constraint and sincerity.

"Style," says E. B. White, "is the sound of words on paper." The manner in which carefully chosen words are used in sentences and distributed in paragraphs, however attractively arranged, will not compensate for content or integrity. Everyone appreciates cultivated graces and skills that come with study and experience, but genuineness of character and purpose are not synonymous with correct format.

Some correspondents prefer the block-style arrangement of a letter, with the address, salutation, message, complimentary close and signature forming a straight line to the left, while others use indented paragraphs with the date and signature falling in a line from the center of the letterhead. Many writers use their initials and those of the transcriber in the lower left-hand corner of the letter (for instance, GCJ:rlb). This is general practice in business and government correspondence. Other equally busy people prefer to identify their letters by less formal indications. This can be accomplished by marking the carbons.

SUMMARY

It is generally agreed that there should be a summary sentence or paragraph to emphasize reaction to a proposal or to reiterate one's point of view. This need not be long and may be accomplished in several ways. Here are some courteous sentences designed to cause the reader to reflect on the letter and prepare him for the complimentary close.

You may be assured of my cooperation, if it is at all possible.

After you have had an opportunity to read these very brief and sketchy materials, I should like to discuss the matter of church membership with you.

We are glad to have you and your wife attending our church, and it would be good to have you in our fellowship.

Please feel free to share with me any problems that might arise, and be assured of my assistance and that of the staff.

I commend these fine people to you and trust that you may have an opportunity to see them soon.

Unless you consent to this suit, it then seems that the whole matter will have to be dropped and the suit heretofore filed would have to be dismissed without consummating the sale of your interest.

We are looking forward to a great convention in Washington and trust that you will not only attend but will be instrumental in leading others to be present.

Knowing of your interest, I will keep you advised.

Again my congratulations on your appointment. My good wishes to you in your new job, and should I ever be able to assist you, feel free to call.

Please command me for any additional information which I may be able to furnish.

COMPLIMENTARY CLOSE

The close of a letter should be consistent with content, style, and tone. One would scarcely use "Very truly yours" in concluding a congratulatory message, nor would he write "I'll be seeing you" at the end of a note of condolence. Moreover, one should avoid such hackneyed phrases as "Thanking you in advance," "I remain," "Trusting this meets with your approval," "See you in church," and "Yours in Christ."

A fresher and more personal approach is always desirable. The following suggestions may prove to be helpful guides.

To a friend:

> With appreciation for our friendship, I am
> Cordially,

To a stranger:

> With all good wishes, I am
> Sincerely,

To one who has befriended you:

>   Gratefully and sincerely,

To an official:

>   Yours very sincerely,

To a member of your church:

>   With pastoral good wishes, I am
>   Sincerely,

To a casual business acquaintance:

>   Thanking you for bringing the matter to my attention, I am
>   Cordially yours,

To a celebrity:

>   Yours very respectfully,
> *or*
>   Most sincerely yours,
> *or*
>   Respectfully yours.

To a relative:

>   With all good wishes for the holidays, I am
>   Affectionately,

SIGNATURES

Whatever the nature of the communication, it should be properly signed. If the letter is worth writing, it merits the author's signature. Assuming it is typed, the sender should type his name and position in the company, institution, or church below the complimentary close, leaving ample space for signature. Many of us write so poorly that it is most helpful to have the name typed below the signature! Should one be unable to sign a letter, it would be proper to add a postscript reading, "Dictated—not signed."

In closing letters to women, men should use such phrases as "sincerely," and "respectfully," thus avoiding "cordially yours." In writing to men, women should use "sincerely" instead of "yours" and "yours truly."

To sign a letter "Edith Brown" does not convey marital status to an unacquainted reader. It is preferable, therefore, to use "Miss" before the signature if the writer is single. Married women should use not only the title "Mrs." but the entire name, that is, Mrs. John Thomas Smith below the signature, Edith Brown Smith. In the case of a divorcée, the name should be signed Mrs. Edith Brown Smith, assuming that the maiden name is Brown. No parenthesis is necessary. Titles and degrees in most cases are not considered a part of a regular signature and should be omitted.

3

Church Correspondence

While a common resemblance and purpose is to be found in all correspondence, that of the church differs in that it communicates the good will of the Christian community to other communities and individuals. Church correspondence is distinctive, for, above all, it seeks to communicate the truth and spirit of Jesus Christ. Therefore it must represent the best not only in materials and methods but also in taste and tone.

"The truth is, I need a letter every ten minutes to encourage me and silence my guilty conscience. I don't like myself well enough —though I admire myself enormously—to expect anyone else to like me." [1] One cannot read the correspondence between Mrs. Patrick Campbell and George Bernard Shaw without seriously considering Shaw's evaluation of a letter: "Remember that only on paper has humanity yet achieved glory, beauty, truth, knowledge, virtue and abiding love."

Nowhere are these truths more evident than in church correspondence, especially in that of a minister. Most parishioners need a letter "every ten minutes" to keep them going, not to mention the

---

[1] Alan Dent (ed.), *Bernard Shaw and Mrs. Patrick Campbell: Their Correspondence* (New York: Alfred A. Knopf, 1952. London: Victor Gollancz, 1952), p. 63. Used by permission of the estate of Mrs. Patrick Campbell.

vast and invisible congregation which is constantly approaching the pastor for counsel and assistance. Every clergyman has the unique privilege of communicating encouragement, truth, comfort, and confidence. Particularly a minister of a city church is overwhelmed with general correspondence requiring an inconceivable amount of time, diplomacy, and energy.

Letter writing is the minister's perpetual pulpit! Correspondence is not a gimmick of the modern church. Leaders and workers throughout the centuries have used the medium of the letter to communicate the message of Jesus Christ. This intimate Christian commerce between minds, hearts, and communities had its origin in the early church, beginning with the letters of Paul.

A FIRST CENTURY CORRESPONDENT

In his thrilling correspondence Paul ran the gamut from encouragement to condemnation, from theological subjects to the details of his personal schedule, from the glory of spiritual victories to the incongruities of professing Christians. Long before there were church buildings or organizations, this Apostle was promulgating and promoting the Christian faith through the medium of written words. One marvels at the diversity of his style and the depth of his perception.

This pioneer missionary was concerned for all the churches, and he was forever in correspondence with them. His personal letters were addressed to the various needs of the Christian communities as he saw them. The direct intimate style of Paul suggests that the majority of his letters (Romans and the 13th and 15th chapters of First Corinthians seem to have been premeditated and carefully polished) were hurriedly dictated to a scribe.

Paul was a voluminous correspondent. The actual number of letters attributed to him varies. Readers of the King James Version of the Scriptures will find some fourteen letters ascribed to this "Pharisee of the Pharisees." Other scholars claim thirteen; still others agree there is a "remarkable nucleus of Pauline writings" in the New Testament. There is rather widespread agreement, I think, that First and Second Thessalonians, Galatians, First and Second Corinthians, Romans, Philippians, Colossians, and Philemon are

definitely by Paul. Although Ephesians, First and Second Timothy, and Titus resemble Paul in personality and style, it is generally felt that Paul is not their author.

The format of Paul's letters followed rather closely the accepted pattern of the day.

> *The Salutation:* Paul, to the church at _____
> *Thanksgiving and Prayer:* I thank God always . . .
> *Doctrinal Discussion of the Subject in Hand:* For I would have you know . . .
> *Practical Application of the Principles Discussed:* Walk worthily . . .
> *Personal Greetings:* The brethren that are with me salute you . . .
> *Benediction:* The Grace of the Lord Jesus Christ be with your Spirit.[2]

Establishing the church at Thessalonica was difficult. It would seem that the burden of the Thessalonian correspondence is that of thanksgiving for their faithfulness and encouragement. We can learn much from this early letter addressed to a congregation:

Paul, Silvanus, and Timothy,
To the church of the Thessalonians in God the Father and the Lord Jesus Christ:
Grace to you and peace.

We give thanks to God always for you all, constantly mentioning you in our prayers, remembering before our God and Father your work of faith and labor of love and steadfastness of hope in our Lord Jesus Christ. For we know, brethren beloved by God, that he has chosen you; for our gospel came to you not only in word, but also in power and in the Holy Spirit and with full conviction. You know what kind of men we proved to be among you for your sake. And you became imitators of us and of the Lord, for you received the word in much affliction, with joy inspired by the Holy Spirit; so that you became an example to all the believers in Macedonia and in Achaia. For not only has the word of the Lord sounded forth from you in Macedonia and Achaia, but your faith in God has gone forth everywhere, so that we need not say anything. For they themselves report concerning us what a

[2] Chester Warren Quimby, *Paul for Everyone* (New York: The Macmillan Company, 1958), pp. 57–58. Used by permission.

welcome we had among you, and how you turned to God from idols, to serve a living and true God, and to wait for his Son from heaven, whom he raised from the Dead, Jesus who delivers us from the wrath to come. (I Thessalonians I R.S.V.)

The letter to Philemon is *personal*. It is sent to the master of a slave by the name of Onesimus. It is steeped in the spirit of Christ. Adroitly Paul appeals for leniency for the runaway slave. The writer refers to himself as "a prisoner for Christ Jesus." The question of slavery was involved and afforded the courageous apostle an opportunity to speak of freedom.

Paul, a prisoner for Christ Jesus, and Timothy our brother,
To Philemon our beloved fellow worker and Apphia our sister and Archippus our fellow soldier, and the church in your house:
Grace to you and peace from God our Father and the Lord Jesus Christ.

I thank my God always when I remember you in my prayers, because I hear of your love and of the faith which you have toward the Lord Jesus and all the saints, and I pray that the sharing of your faith may promote the knowledge of all the good that is ours in Christ. For I have derived much joy and comfort from your love, my brother, because the hearts of the saints have been refreshed through you.
Accordingly, though I am bold enough in Christ to command you to do what is required, yet for love's sake I prefer to appeal to you—I, Paul, an ambassador and now a prisoner also for Christ Jesus—I appeal to you for my child, Onesimus, whose father I have become in my imprisonment. (Formerly he was useless to you, but now he is indeed useful to you and to me.) I am sending him back to you, sending my very heart. I would have been glad to keep him with me, in order that he might serve me on your behalf during my imprisonment for the gospel; but I preferred to do nothing without your consent in order that your goodness might not be by compulsion but of your own free will.
Perhaps this is why he was parted from you for a while, that you might have him back for ever, no longer as a slave but more than a slave, as a beloved brother, especially to me but how much more to you, both in the flesh and in the Lord. So if you consider me your partner, receive him as you would receive me. If he has wronged you at all, or owes you anything, charge that to my ac-

count. I, Paul, write this with my own hand, I will repay it—to say nothing of your owing me even your own self. Yes, brother, I want some benefit from you in the Lord. Refresh my heart in Christ.

Confident of your obedience, I write to you, knowing that you will do even more than I say. At the same time, prepare a guest room for me, for I am hoping through your prayers to be granted to you.

Epaphras, my fellow prisoner in Christ Jesus, sends greetings to you, and so do Mark, Aristarchus, Demas, and Luke, my fellow workers.

The grace of the Lord Jesus Christ be with your spirit.[3]

Not all of Paul's missives are so brief and so compassionate. Some are long and involved. Many deal with difficult questions of doctrine and theology. Paul was not only a peacemaker but a profound thinker. He addressed himself to people, discussing problems, churches, sin, injuries, rulers, power, death, resurrection, and salvation. As an example of the way Paul handled these subjects, read his inspiring account of the resurrection in the Fifteenth Chapter of First Corinthians. Certainly it is the most erudite, informative, and inspiring letter ever written about immortality.

A FIFTH CENTURY SAINT

The fifth century bishop of Hippo, St. Augustine, is remembered for many contributions to the church, not the least being his letters.

To the Members of Christ, my well-beloved and much longed for lords of the holy congregation to which I minister, Augustine sends greetings in the Lord.

Your devotion, my holy brethren, to our Lord Jesus Christ, well known to me and often tested, has given me, though absent, reason to place reliance in that wherein I have been wont to rejoice when present: in spirit I am always with you, not only because the great sweetness of the grace of our Lord Jesus Christ ever continueth its fragrance, but also because you do not suffer me, who am your servant in the Gospel, to endure any hardship.

[3] The Letter of Paul to Philemon (R.S.V.).

Now, our brother Fascius was being pressed for payment of a debt of seventeen solidi by the tribute-gatherers and found for the moment no way of escape from his entanglement; wherefore, so as not to suffer bodily injury, he fled to the protection of Holy Church. And as those tax-collectors were compelled to take their departure and so were unable to grant him a respite, they heaped on me the most grievous abuse, declaring that I ought to hand him over to them or to furnish the means wherefrom they could receive the debt which they proved was owing them. I made the offer to Fascius to speak to you, holy brethren, about his needs, but, deterred by shame, he implored me not to do it. So I myself, under pressure of greater needs, accepted seventeen solidi from our brother Macedonius, and these I immediately handed over on his behalf, while he promised that on a certain day he could meet the repayment, and agreed that if he was not able to meet it, an appeal should be made for him to that compassion of yours, which it is your habit to display as a brotherly feeling for our brethren.

Wherefore, now that he is absent, it remains for you to give your backing, not to him, for no one can apply compulsion to him in his absence, but to my promise, for with you my good name and fame are always present. For already the day on which he promised he would meet the debt, is past and gone, and I find no reply to make to him who gave me the amount on trust, save to do what I promised I would do. But since I had no information about this matter on the day of Pentecost, so that I might have made an appeal when the crowd at Church was greater than usual, I ask you to be good enough to take this letter as my voice, while in your hearts Our Lord and God speaks warning and exhortation; in Him you have put your trust, and He never leaves us so long as we fear and honour His name; in Him I too am united with you, although in body I seem to have departed from you; from Him comes the promise of the harvest of eternal life from this seed of good works, for the apostle says: "And let us not be weary in welldoing, for in due season we shall reap if we faint not. As we therefore have opportunity, let us do good unto all men, especially unto them who are of the household of faith." Since then he is of the household of faith, a member of the Christian Church, a Catholic brother of our own, for the satisfaction of whose needs I ask you to do what the Lord bids you do, do it without grudging, without complaint, and with gladness and cheerfulness; for your trust is in God, not in man, and He has promised that you will lose nothing of the things you do in mercy, but will receive them on that day with eternal usury. And since the apostle himself says "But this I say, He which soweth sparingly shall reap also sparingly," you should understand that now is the time for us, while we are still in this life, to purchase with haste and cheerfulness the gift of eternal life; for when the end of the world comes, it will be given only to those who through faith have bought it for themselves before it was possible for them to see it.

I have written to the priests as well that, if there be any deficiency after the offering made by you, my holy friends, they should make it up from the Church's store, provided that you have all made cheerful offering, each man as he will; for whether the gift come from you or from the Church, it is all God's, yet your devotedness will be far more acceptable than the treasures of the Church, as the apostle says, "Not because I desire a gift, but I desire that fruit may abound." Gladden my heart, then, for I wish to have joy of your fruits; for you are God's trees which even through my ministry he deigns to water with unceasing showers. May the Lord keep you from all evil, both in this world, and in the world to come, my well-beloved lords and much longed for brethren.[4]

A FIFTEENTH CENTURY CHURCHMAN

History is filled with correspondence of Christians seeking to experience spiritual encounter and to communicate eternal values. Those who have loved and served the church through the centuries have voiced their complaints and commitments. Many considered John Huss to be a heretic. Some of his most trenchant correspondence was from his cell before he was led to the stake, July 6, 1415. You will want to examine this letter:

A multitude of people have come to exhort me, and amongst them many doctors, but few brethren, as the Apostle has said. They were prodigal in their counsels and phrases; they told me, that I could and I ought to abjure my scruples in submitting my will to the Holy Church, which the Council represents; but not one of them can avoid the difficulty, when I place him in my situation,

[4] From *St. Augustine, Select Letters*, with English translation by James Houston Baxter. (Cambridge: Loeb Classical Library and Harvard University Press, 1930), pp. 521–527. Used by permission.

and ask him, if, being certain of having never preached, or defended, or entertained heresy, he could, in safe conscience, formally confess that he abjured an error which he never supported. Some of them stated, that it was not necessary to abjure, but merely to renounce the heresy held or not held; others maintain, that to abjure signifies to deny what is attested rightly or erroneously. I would willingly swear, I replied to them, that I have never preached, held, or defended, the errors which are imputed to me; and that I will never preach, hold, or defend them. And when I spoke thus, they immediately retired.

Others insist that, supposing a man really innocent were found in the Church, and this man, through humility, confess himself guilty, he would be well deserving; thereupon some one cited, amongst the ancient fathers, a certain saint, in whose bed had been covertly put a prohibited book. Inculpated and examined on this subject, the saint denied the fault, but his enemies answered, "Thou hast concealed the book, and put it in thy bed;" and this book having been found there, the saint confessed himself culpable. Some supported this opinion by the example of a certain holy woman, who lived in a monastery in the disguise of a man. She was accused of being the father of a child. She confessed it, and kept the child: her innocence was afterwards discovered with her sex. Many other means were also proposed to me.

An Englishman addressed me thus, "Were I in your place, I would abjure; for in England, all the masters, and all men held in consideration, who were suspected of adhering to the opinions of Wycliffe, have been severally cited before the archbishop and have abjured."

Lastly, yesterday they were all agreed in engaging me to place myself at the mercy of the Council.

Paletz came at my entreaty, for I desired to confess to him. I asked the commissioners, and those who exhorted me, to give me for confessor either him or another. And I said, "Paletz is my principal adversary: I wish to confess to him; or, at least, give me in his stead a man qualified to hear me: I conjure you to do so in the name of the Lord." This last desire was accorded: I confessed to a monk, who piously and most patiently listened to me; he gave me absolution, and counselled me, but did not enjoin me, to follow the advice of others.

Paletz came: he wept with me when I besought him to pardon me for having uttered before him some offensive words, and especially for having called him a forger of writings. And as I reminded him that, in a public audience, when he heard me deny the articles cited by the witnesses, he rose up and cried: "This man does not believe in God,"—he denied it, but truly he said it, and perhaps you heard him do so. I reminded him, in what manner he said to me in prison, in presence of the Commissioners, "Since the birth of Christ, no heretic has written more dangerously than Wycliffe and thou." He also insisted, that all those who have read my sermons are infected with the error concerning the sacrament of the altar. He has now denied it, adding, "I did not say all, but a great number." And yet it is certain that he said it. And when I took him up by saying, "Oh! Master Paletz, how much you wrong me in accusing my auditory of heresy!" he did not reply anything, and he exhorted me, like the others, always repeating, that through me and mine much harm had been done. He told me, also that he possessed a letter addressed to the Bohemians, in which was written, that, at the Chateau, I sang some verses on my captivity. In the name of Heaven, take great care of my letters: do not let them be carried to any clerical person, and let our seigniors only trust some laymen. Inform me whether they accompany the Emperor. Jesus Christ, by his grace, preserves me unmoveable in my first resolution.

JOHN HUSS, in hope, servant of God.[5]

A SEVENTEENTH CENTURY BISHOP

The letters of St. Francis de Sales, Bishop of Geneva from 1602 to 1622, reveal his perception of the problems faced by the people he served. Despite demands imposed upon him by duties in the Court of King Henry IV, he took time to write letters of encouragement to those striving to keep their faith alive.

To MADAME DE LA FLECHERE:

ANNECY, April or May, 1608
I have been much consoled by the letters you have written to me and by seeing that Our Lord has let you taste the beginnings of that tranquillity with which, by the help of his grace, we must

[5] From *Letters of John Huss Written During His Exile and Imprisonment*, with Martin Luther's Preface, Emile de Bonnechose, translated by C. Mackenzie (Edinburgh: William Whyte & Co., 1846). Reprinted by permission of E. P. Dutton & Co., Inc. from *The Great Prisoners*, edited by Isidore Abramowitz (New York: E. P. Dutton & Co., Inc., 1946), pp. 73–74.

from now on continue to serve him in the rush and variety of business forced on us by our vocation. I have very great hopes for you because I think I have seen your heart firmly resolved to serve his divine Majesty in the exercises of devotion. And if it happens that you often fail because of infirmity, you must not be in any way put out; but while hating the offence towards God, you must also cultivate a certain joyful humility which helps you to make a point of seeing and recognizing your misery.

I will tell you briefly what exercises I advise for you; you will see them set out more fully in something else that I wrote. Preparation for the whole day which is done briefly in the morning, mental prayer before dinner, which can take an hour or thereabouts according to your leisure; in the evening, before supper, a short time of recollection during which by way of repetition you will make a few heart-felt aspirations to God on your morning meditation, or some other subject.

During the day and amidst your work, examine yourself as often as you can to see whether your love is not too far engaged in what you are doing, or in some way out of order, and whether your hand is still clasped in that of Our Lord. If you find yourself harassed beyond measure, calm and quieten your spirit. Imagine how Our Lady calmly used one hand to do what needed doing while she held her Child with her other hand or on her other arm, for she held him most carefully.

In time of peace and tranquillity make many acts of meekness, for in this way you will tame your heart and train it to gentleness. Do not stop to fight the small temptations which come your way by contesting them or disputing with them, but simply by turning your heart back to Jesus Christ crucified, as though kissing his side or his feet because you love him.

Do not force yourself to much vocal prayer; and when you are praying and feel your heart carried towards mental prayer, always let it follow this attraction freely. And if you were to use mental prayer only, together with the Lord's prayer, the Hail Mary and the creed, that would do perfectly well.

I dedicate myself whole-heartedly to the service of your soul which will henceforward be as dear to me as my own. May Our Lord rule for ever, and I am in him your servant,

FRANCIS, *Bishop of Geneva* [6]

⁶ Elisabeth Stopp, *St. Francis de Sales, Selected Letters* (New York: Harper & Brothers), pp. 150–151. Copyright 1960 by Elisabeth Stopp. Used by permission.

TWENTIETH CENTURY CHRISTIAN

Dietrich Bonhoeffer was wellborn. His father, a physician, taught psychiatry at Berlin University. Later a student at the university, Dietrich struggled between giving himself to science or theology. Dialectical theology won. Eventually he served the Confessing Church in Germany. War was imminent. Those who recognized his splendid mind and spirit desperately tried to protect him from the inevitable involvements with Nazism. He declined sanctuary and preached the gospel until he was arrested by the Gestapo, April 5, 1943. While in a concentration camp he made friends with fellow prisoners, orderlies, and guards who frequently apologized for having to lock him in at night. The guards were among those who smuggled out of prison his now famous papers and letters. Thus another prisoner of Christ and servant of the church wrote heroically to a friend.

July 21st, 1944

All I want to do today is to send you a short greeting. I expect you are always pleased to hear we are still alive, even if we lay aside our theological discussion for the moment. It's true these theological problems are always occupying my mind, but there are times when I am just content to live the life of faith without worrying about its problems. In such moods I take a simple pleasure in the text of the day, and yesterday's and today's were particularly good (July 20th: Psalm 20.8: Romans 8.31; July 21st: Psalm 23.1: John 10.24). Then I go back to Paul Gerhardt's wonderful hymns, which never pall.

During the last year or so I have come to appreciate the "worldliness" of Christianity as never before. The Christian is not a *homo religiosus*, but a man, pure and simple, just as Jesus was a man, compared with John the Baptist anyhow. I don't mean the shallow this-worldliness of the enlightened, of the busy, the comfortable or the lascivious. It's something much more profound than that, something in which the knowledge of death and resurrection is ever present. I believe Luther lived a this-worldly life in this sense. I remember talking to a young French pastor at A. thirteen years ago. We were discussing what our real purpose was in life. He said he would like to become a saint. I think it is quite likely he did become one. At the time I was very much impressed, though I disagreed with him, and said I should prefer to have faith, or words to that effect. For a long time I did not realize how far we were apart. I thought I could acquire faith by trying to live a holy life, or something like it. It was in this phase that I wrote *The Cost of Discipleship.* Today I can see the dangers of this book, though I am prepared to stand by what I wrote.

Later I discovered and am still discovering up to this very moment that it is only by living completely in this world that one learns to believe. One must abandon every attempt to make something of oneself, whether it be a saint, a converted sinner, a churchman (the priestly type, so called!) a righteous man or an unrighteous one, a sick man or a healthy one. This is what I mean by worldliness—taking life in one's stride, with all its duties and problems, its successes and failures, its experience and helplessness. It is in such a life that we throw ourselves utterly into the arms of God and participate in His sufferings in the world and watch with Christ in Gethsemane. That is faith, that is *metanoia,* and that is what makes a man and a Christian (cf. Jeremiah 45). How can success make us arrogant or failure lead us astray, when we participate in the sufferings of God by living in this world?

I think you get my meaning, though I put it so briefly. I am glad I have been able to learn it, and I know I could only have done so along the road I have travelled. So I am grateful and content with the past and the present. Perhaps you are surprised at the personal tone of this letter, but if for once I want to talk like this, to whom else should I say it? May God in his mercy lead us through these times. But above all may he lead us to himself!

I was delighted to hear from you, and glad you aren't finding it too hot. There must still be many letters from me on the way. Did we travel more or less along that way in 1936?

Good-bye. Take care of yourself and don't lose hope—we shall all meet again soon! [7]

A LETTER FROM THE CONGO

While the world was focusing on the political crises in Congo, missionaries were evacuated. During this tense period, when many

[7] Dietrich Bonhoeffer, *Prisoner for God* (New York: The Macmillan Company, 1953), pp. 168–169. Copyright 1953 by The Macmillan Company. Published in Great Britain under the title *Letters and Papers from Prison* by Student Christian Movement Press, Ltd. Used by permission.

young churches were stripped of their leadership, the Congolese Christians expressed their gratitude for the missionaries and their faith in the future of the church.

BOLENGE, August 5, 1960

TO OUR DEVOTED MISSIONARIES:

Since your departure following the sad and grievous events through which we all suffered during many days, we have never ceased to pray for you, for the church and for ourselves. Your departure seemed to us necessary and imperative. It has saved, we believe, the life of the young church of Congo and its honor before the Missionary Societies of Congo, Europe and America. Certainly this departure has dearly cost the Missionary Societies, but this price will have its effect on the future of the Congo. We are with you all in this sad departure, in your happiness of service to your Master and Savior and in your joy to belong to the flock of God.

We pray constantly that God, through his divine wisdom, will direct the Congolese people to restore peace in the country with the utmost rapidity through the instrument of the UN. We cast our eyes toward God to hope for your prompt return in the interest of the Church of Christ in Congo. We are facing a new structure in this country for which you have given your best. This change in the politics of the country calls for strong and loyal Christians who, according to the words of the Lord Jesus, will truly be the "salt" and the "light" of the new Congo. Now more than ever the Protestant churches and missions must redouble their efforts. Working together in the great principles of the gospel of Christ, with tolerance for the little differences of interpretations and of customs in our daily lives, according to the example of Jesus Christ and above all in brotherly love. This must serve more and more as a base orientation of the Congo toward a grand empire whose fundamental law is the knowledge of God.

May God hear our prayers and grant them. May the grace of the Savior, Jesus Christ, the love of the Father and the Communion of the Holy Spirit be with us all and with each one in particular.[8]

[8] Letter by official representatives of the Congo Church in the Coquilhatville-Bolenge area, *Leaven*, Vol. XIII, No. 3, October, 1960. United Christian Missionary Society, Indianapolis. Used by permission.

Whatever the century or the concern, the Christian letter breathes truth, kindness, and affection. It is free of commercial clichés. It is not a merchandising piece. It is honest sharing, a transcribed conversation addressed to conscience, mind, and heart.

4

Letters of Administration

Good letter writing is so essential to the successful conduct of business that many institutions and firms are experimenting in this field. For instance, one company brings in an expert correspondent to conduct classes in letter writing. Another retains letter-writing counselors and consultants. In this situation, management personnel are brought together for a series of workshop sessions in effective writing. A course in the fundamentals and skills of correspondence is taught once a week for three hours and continues over a period of six weeks.

The management of still another company is encouraged to—

want to write better letters.
appreciate the satisfaction that comes from skill in self-expression.
understand the real goals of business writing so they can measure
    their own standards of performance against the goals.
get rid of bad writing habits and develop good ones.[1]

This should do much to stimulate additional interest in the art of written communication.

[1] *Better Business Writing*, Southwestern Bell Telephone Company, St. Louis. Used by permission.

Though the church is far more than a visible organization, its program must be efficiently administered. Church administration is a reversible coin. While the demands of a given parish largely determine the caliber and versatility of its leadership, the leadership of a church, nonetheless, gives vision and vitality to its program. Intelligent and effective communications are the foundations of sound administration.

Like every well conducted institution, a church must have orderly and democratically acceptable methods of arriving at decisions and implementing the wishes of the majority. This is the quintessence of good program planning. Once this is established, it becomes the responsibility of the staff to prepare the congregation for enthusiastic participation. Some member of the staff, usually the minister, must set the tone of communications and observe ever so carefully the calendar of timing. The skillful letter is an indispensable line of communication in the vortex of church administration. Its clarity, warmth, and challenge may be the difference between mediocre and excellent churchmanship.

ANNOUNCEMENT

A common and ever-recurring form of correspondence is the letter of announcement. Its major purpose is to call attention to some forthcoming event, arouse interest, and seek cooperation. This type of letter appears so simple that frequently it is lifeless and consequently ineffectual. In the following announcement letters you will note the difference in style, format, and psychology as well as length.

Anniversary Service

September, 1960

DEAR FRIENDS OF ST. MARK'S:

I was four years old when it happened. The Archduke Ferdinand had not yet been assassinated at Sarajevo, and the First World War had not begun. The world was still the "old" world of prosperity and peace. Four more years were to pass before the lights all over Europe began to go out and the stage of the world was darkened for the first act of a tremendous, tragic drama. Since then we have seen and survived Act II of that same tragedy and many are wondering whether we are not now nearing the end of the restless interval before the opening of the third and final act. The principal actors—the United States, the British Commonwealth, France, Belgium, Germany and Russia—are still involved, though with some changes of name, character and costume; but the revolving stage of the world is now set for the "crowd scenes" and the multitudes of Africa, Asia and India are adding their dark colors to the scene and their turmoil to the conflict and confusion.

But on the day of which I speak, and which some few of you can well remember, all this was in the unknown, unanticipated future; and on that day, the 29th day of September in the year 1910, an event took place of which it might also be said that "the world took little note nor long remembered." A magnificent gothic church in the city of Minneapolis was dedicated to the glory of God and in honor of St. Mark the Evangelist. The erection of St. Mark's on the loveliest site in the city was an outward and visible sign and witness of an inward and spiritual faith and trust in God—a vote of confidence in the future. We are now in what was the future then; and though we may feel that faith and trust in God came easier in those spacious days of fifty years ago, yet always it is the time of trial that tests and either makes or breaks our faith in God and in our fellowmen. But the light of a match can be seen farther by night than the most powerful searchlight in sunshine. The charge and the challenge of the 50th anniversary of the dedication of Saint Mark's is clear and inescapable. "Other men labored, and we have entered into their labors," and, by the faithful witness of our public worship as well as the integrity of our personal lives, our bounden duty is to let our light—which is the reflected light of Christ—so shine before men that they may see our good works and glorify our Father who is in Heaven. Freely indeed we have received; freely, if we are to remain free, we must give.

It is my earnest hope and prayer not only that the anniversary services on Sunday, October 2, will all be well attended, but also that the occasion will mark a renewal and a rededication of ourselves to face the challenge of the years ahead.

Yours very sincerely; [2]

[2] Written by The Very Reverend Henry N. Hancock, The Cathedral Church of St. Mark, Minneapolis. Used by permission.

Reformation Day

The following communication was directed to ministers whose churches participated in the Church Federation.

September 15, 1960

DEAR FRIEND:

May I have two minutes of your time for a matter of great importance to Protestantism in the Metropolitan area?

A totally new observance of Reformation Day is planned for October 30 this year. The Board of the Metropolitan Church Federation approved the plan last Friday and now we submit it to you with a most urgent request for your participation. There will be no mass meeting at Kiel Auditorium this year.

The plan calls for each congregation to observe the day at its own services with the following things in common:

1. Each pastor to preach a sermon with the same title, "Here I Stand"; the text: Galatians 5:1.
2. A full-page advertisement in each of the two major newspapers. Enclosure will be full-page size and will include the name of your local church.
3. A bulletin insert (to be sent to you in the number you order on the return card) having the Reformation statement on one side and a responsive reading on the other side.
4. A contribution from your Church toward the expense, in the amount of $10, $15, $25 or $50. Your participation and inclusion in the listed churches will not depend on a contribution, but the full-page advertisement *will depend on enough gifts*.

The use of a common sermon subject (the sermon to be anything you are led to preach under that title), the common advertising and a common effort at large attendance in each church will involve all our people and present a solid Protestant front in Metropolitan Saint Louis. The success of this common effort depends on your personal cooperation.

Please return the enclosed postal card indicating the elements of this plan in which you will participate, the number of bulletin inserts you need and the amount of the contribution you will send.

Thank you for your help and prompt response. Our Reformation Day impact depends on you.

Faithfully yours,[3]

Projection of Meetings and Dates

November 22, 1960

To: *Members of the Department of Stewardship and Benevolence*
Re: *Dates in 1961*

DEAR COLLEAGUES:

You have just secured your new 1961 appointment book and before your calendar is filled with other appointments I wish to lay claim to the following dates on behalf of the cause of Christian stewardship:

February 9–11	Conference on Modern Christian Philanthropy, Sheraton-Cleveland Hotel, Cleveland, Ohio.
February 16–18	Consultation on the Church as Employer, Money Raiser, and Investor, Warwick Estates, Warwick, New York, sponsored by the Department of The Church and Economic Life. (For inquiry of interest, write the Department of Stewardship and Benevolence.)
March 22	Executive Committee of the Department of Stewardship and Benevolence meeting in New York.
April 5–7	Workshop on World Stewardship Concerns, sponsored jointly by the Division of Foreign Missions and the Department of Stewardship and Benevolence.
July 9–12	Workshop for Capital-Funds Administrators, Conference Point Camp, Williams Bay, Wisconsin, sponsored by the Department of Stewardship and Benevolence.
July 12	Executive Committee of the Department of Stewardship and Benevolence, Conference Point Camp, Williams Bay, Wisconsin.

[3] Written by Dr. W. Sherman Skinner, Minister, Second Presbyterian Church, St. Louis, and Chairman, Reformation Commission, Metropolitan Church Federation of Greater St. Louis. Used by permission.

July 12–15   Conference on Every Member Canvass Techniques, Conference Point Camp, Williams Bay, Wisconsin.

August 31 to   Conference on Stewardship, Ecumenical In-
September 6   stitute, Bossey, Switzerland. (For information write the Department of Stewardship and Benevolence. Nominations are made by the Department, but actual invitations are issued by the World Council of Churches.)

December 11–15   Annual Meeting of the Department of Stewardship and Benevolence, Buck Hill Falls, Pennsylvania.

Please note that in 1962 a Workshop on World Stewardship Concerns is being suggested for July to follow up the Bossey experience, the World Council meetings in New Delhi in December 1961, and the visit of the Executive Director during 1961 and 1962.

Further information regarding these meetings will be sent to you as plans develop.

Most cordially yours,[4]

Questionnaires

The minister must devote discreet and prompt attention to the wide variety of questionnaires which come to his desk, ranging from graduate students seeking data for their theses to morticians conducting surveys.

May 23, 1961

DEAR DR. JONES:

In all phases of our life, the church is the only institution in the world which continually serves us. As infants we are baptized; as children we are taught the lessons of life in the church school; as adults we come to the church to be married. In times of great need, we turn to the church for comfort, help and guidance. In death we look to the church for spiritual guidance. The staff of Lupton Chapel feels privileged to work closely with the clergymen in helping people in this trying hour.

---

[4] Written by Dr. T. K. Thompson, Executive Director, Department of Stewardship and Benevolence, Division of Christian Life and Work, National Council of the Churches of Christ, New York. Used by permission.

To better serve our families in their time of need, we feel that we should know more of the clergyman's thinking on various phases of funeral practices. Would you take a few moments and express your opinion about funerals? This is a confidential survey and you need not sign the questionnaire. We are only interested in opinions. Should there be any particular problem, we'll be glad to discuss the matter with you. We feel that any improvement that we can make in funeral service will benefit all. Probably a good starting point is the relationship between the clergyman and funeral director.

We thank you for your cooperation. If you are interested in a majority analysis of the questionnaire, we'll be glad to send you our findings.

Very truly yours,[5]

The questionnaire from this splendid firm consisted of fifty questions, among them:

Do you prefer to be addressed as Doctor, Reverend, Pastor, or Mr.? _____

Do you prefer to be called first by the family before the Funeral Director is notified of the death? Yes_____No_____ Indifferent _____

Do you think the casket should be opened in the church? Yes_____ No_____

Do you believe more information should be provided about funeral costs? Yes_____No_____

Would you like to discuss funeral costs with a reliable Funeral Director? Yes_____No_____Indifferent_____

In your opinion, are Funeral Directors in general cold and commercial or sympathetic and understanding toward those families they serve?_____

Is there any grief therapy or psychological benefit to a funeral service? Yes_____No_____

[5] By C. R. Lupton, Jr., C. R. Lupton & Sons, Morticians, St. Louis. Used by permission.

Do you feel that a family should do financially as they like for a funeral service? Yes_____No_____

Do you think a clergyman should dictate what a funeral should cost the family? Yes_____No_____

Do you prefer a Memorial type service? Yes_____No_____

As a clergyman, do you feel that when we lower the value of an individual in life or death, we undermine the very foundations of our society? Yes_____No_____

Comment: _____

_____

Is there a trend for ministers to become too professional, too scientific or too impersonal? Yes_____No_____

What is your greatest criticism of a Funeral Director?_____

_____

(Use back of sheet for additional comment)

Was William E. Gladstone, former Prime Minister of Great Britain, correct when he said, "Show me the manner in which a nation or a community cares for its dead and I will measure with mathematical exactness the tender sympathies of its people, their respect for the law of the land and their loyalty to high ideals." Yes_____No_____. Are there any general comments that you care to make about funeral services? [6]

TRANSMITTAL

Every administrator must prepare letters of transmittal. This communication is more specific than the general letter of announcement. A letter of transmittal is a covering letter. It substantiates the fact that certain requests have been fulfilled and/or materials enclosed.

[6] Questionnaire prepared by C. R. Lupton & Sons, Morticians, St. Louis. Used by permission.

Concerning Construction

Mr. Fred R. Hammond
c/o Jamieson, Spearl, Hammond, & Grolock, Architects,
Arcade Building
St. Louis 1, Missouri

Subject: Construction of New Heating Plant for Union Avenue
Christian Church

Reference: (a) Your previous negotiations with Dr. Wilbur H. Cramblet

Enclosures: (1) Church's specifications for Heating Plant Equipment dated January 22, 1960 (for combination gas and oil and, as an alternate, per par. h. (2) on Page 3, for gas only equipment)

(2) List of contractors to whom Enclosure (1) specifications were mailed

(3) Quotations on Enclosure (1) specifications from following contractors:
a. Plumbing Serv. Co. dated February 5, 1960
b. Kennedy Heating & Serv. Co., dated February 5, 1960
c. Arco Heating & Eng. Co. (not dated)
d. R & L Waldo, Inc., dated February 4, 1960

(4) Three quotations from Natkin & Co. dated January 12 and 13, 1960, per Church's specifications dated April 28, 1959, somewhat similar to Enclosure (1)

(5) Miscellaneous Contractor information

Dear Mr. Hammond:

Per my telecon today with Dr. Wilbur H. Cramblet, Chairman of the Heating Plant Committee for Union Avenue Christian Church, and in accord with Reference (a) herewith the above-captioned enclosures for your use in preparing drawings and revised specifications for the Church's new heating plant.

For information purposes the following of the above contractors have advised me that they would appreciate an opportunity to furnish a package-type bid for the new plant: viz., including the building and equipment:

Plumbing Service Company
Kennedy Heating & Service Company
R & L Waldo, Inc.

I hope the enclosures will be helpful and I am glad we are again doing business with you.

Sincerely,[7]

Submitting Manuscript

October 14, 1960

Dr. Ralph C. Raughley, Jr.
Editor, Pulpit Digest
159 Northern Blvd.
Great Neck, New York

DEAR DR. RAUGHLEY:

Herewith I submit a sermon for your consideration which was preached recently from the pulpit of our church and which may be worth its space in the *Pulpit Digest*.

Thank you for considering it.

Sincerely,

Money

Salvation Army
122 North 7th Street
St. Louis 1, Missouri

GENTLEMEN:

We are enclosing our check for $103.00 representing contributions of some of our members to the Disaster Relief Fund. Judge Randolph Weber, one of our members who is interested in your organization, suggested that we send the money to you.

Sincerely,[8]

PROMOTIONAL

This type of letter seeks to generate interest in a given project, program, or concern. One might call it one of salesmanship, and it is apt to be lengthy, as it endeavors to present the facts. At a deeper level it is one of real commitment to a worthy cause.

[7] Written by Roy Hansen, Chairman, Policy and Personnel Committee, Union Avenue Christian Church, St. Louis. Used by permission.

[8] Written by O. J. Lloyd, Administrative Assistant, Union Avenue Christian Church, St. Louis. Used by permission.

To Ministers

December 8, 1960

DEAR PASTOR:

I am sure you know that the United Society has conducted a nation-wide campaign during the past eight years known as Capital for Kingdom Building. This special effort was launched in 1953 to provide capital funds for construction of buildings, equipment, transportation units and missionary residence at the seven Home Mission Institutions as well as on the fields overseas.

This campaign found ready acceptance by the churches and has resulted in needed construction and repair that will preserve property and above all add greatly to the effective witness and work of the mission.

For your leadership and the share your congregation has had in Capital for Kingdom Building we are truly appreciative. Missionaries are most generous in their expression of the value of Capital for Kingdom Building. As executive secretary of the Resources and Interpretation Department I wish to personally thank you and members of the congregation for their gifts to Capital for Kingdom Building.

The needs of Capital for Kingdom Building are not completed. During the Decade of Decision we must keep in proper condition and repair what we have done during 1953–1960. However, the promotion of capital funds for mission work is now being coordinated in a united capital asking that it be studied by the two finance commissions and the State Unified Promotion committee. The state in every instance, considers all agency capital funds and presents the total of each agency for the churches to write in their budget along with their regular operating support of world outreach.

It is our hope that the church you serve has United Society Decade Capital in the budget for 1960–61 and will forward this to the Society before June 30, 1961. At the present very, very little has come from the churches, indeed much less than the $522,876.00 received last year. This is alarming, for we had hoped that, responding to the wishes of the churches as expressed in the Listening Conferences for a united effort and less individual agency appeals, the churches would carry over their Capital for Kingdom Building into their present budgets.

For the Decade of Decision the United Society has estimated

its capital and non-recurring needs at $3,907,502. You can see these listed in the "Blueprint" of the Society that has been mailed to you. You will not be receiving Capital for Kingdom Building promotion as in the past, and done so effectively by Mr. Donald Legg. It will be included in the united capital dollar asking for each state. It is, therefore, imperative that in building budget, each local congregation include United Society capital each year during the Decade of Decision and remit at least quarterly.

In closing may I again express sincere appreciation for the gifts made to Capital for Kingdom Building and we shall look forward to receiving your share of the total capital funds dollar in the state from your congregation.

Most cordially,[9]

Choir Rehearsal

> I'll go where you want me to go, dear Lord,
>   Real service is what I desire.
> I'll say what you want me to say, dear Lord,
>   But please don't ask me to sing in the choir.
>
> I'll go where you want me to go, dear Lord,
>   I'll say what you want me to say,
> I'm busy just now with myself, dear Lord,
>   I'll help you some other day.

DEAR CHRISTIAN FRIEND:

I am writing in behalf of your church. Jesus Christ is its Head and you, by faith in Him, are a member of the body—the church. Every member of the body is needed and its abilities are important for particular functions. Every member wants the body to be well and flourishing. We have reasons to believe that you want your church to flourish and to be built up in love.

I am writing to you at this time particularly in behalf of the Senior Choir of your church. If you have been faithful and regular as a member of this choir we say, "Thank you and God bless you." We would encourage you to continue faithful in well doing with the assurance that we deeply appreciate your devoted efforts in this work.

[9] Written by Ira A. Paternoster, Executive Secretary, Department of Resources and Interpretation, United Christian Missionary Society, Indianapolis. Used by permission.

But we need additional choir members. We have often been limping when we should be a well balanced choir of sufficient voices to lead the congregation of God's people in singing praises to our Lord. If you have not yet joined this group, we are at this point speaking to you. You have been pointed out to us as one who has abilities to sing. Your church needs you and wants you to sing in your choir. You believe with us, "that believers, all and every one, . . . must feel himself bound to use his gifts, readily and cheerfully, for the advantage and welfare of other members."— Heidelberg Catechism Question 55. We are saved by grace through faith in Jesus, but how wonderful to know that we may do good works as a means of saying thanks to God and that He will reward them in this life and in that which is to come! What a joy it will be to hear the Lord say to us at last, "Well done, thou good and faithful servant." In anticipation of that joy, we plead with you, "Come over and help us by singing in your church choir— faithfully and regularly." Let us not permit Satan to tempt us away from the service of the Lord.

And that little poem which is at the heading of this letter is sadly true of some but we do not want it to be true for us. And you don't want it to be true for yourself either; do you? By the grace of God, we do want to deny ourselves, take up our cross and follow Jesus. (Matt. 16:24)

We earnestly hope and pray that you will respond to this invitation and come to the next choir rehearsal, or as soon thereafter as possible, and continue faithful in this particular service to your church and its Head, Jesus Christ. Let not this invitation to you be in vain. Personally, I want you to know that by accepting this invitation you will considerably lighten for me the burden of the work of your church and will make unnecessary a personal call on you in behalf of this matter.

Your servant for Christ's sake,[10]

FUND RAISING

No financial campaign could hope to succeed without well conceived and well written letters. Many people need to read a thing in order to fully comprehend it. The written message continues to

[10] Written by Frank Snuttjer, Minister, Salem Reformed Church, Little Rock, Iowa. Used by permission.

penetrate the mind and heart long after verbiage has died away. Direct mailing is a common means of communicating a need and preparing individuals for financial commitment. One should rely on this only where personal confrontation is impossible. The fund-raising letter is a test of psychology, strategy, and skill. Here are some interesting examples:

Alerting Alumni

To Alumni of the Divinity School:
President Griswold's Annual Report to the Alumni this year takes the form of a Special Report on Yale's Program for the Arts and Sciences. It explains why Yale must have additional capital now, in order to maintain its traditional position of leadership. I enclose a copy and commend it to your thoughtful consideration.

This Program has been a long time in the making and many people have participated in its formulation—alumni, faculty, and members of the Yale administration. It seeks to satisfy the needs of Yale College and the Graduate School totalling $69,500,000.

In this Report the President also refers to the University's overall goal of $147,000,000 by 1970, which includes the capital needs of all the professional schools. As the President points out, the success of Yale's Program for the Arts and Sciences will not only speed Yale on her way to her 1970 goal, but will give her the resources she urgently needs to sustain her historic purpose under the extreme pressures and in the difficult circumstances of the present.

The needs of the Divinity School are included in the 1970 goal in the amount of $3,150,000. You will be hearing more about our plans to satisfy these needs, and I know they will have your wholehearted support.

                Sincerely,[11]

Church Budget

                        May 2, 1960

DEAR MEMBER OR FRIEND OF UNION AVENUE:
I am a pledge card. I go into every home in Union Avenue. I

[11] Written by Dr. Liston Pope, Dean, Divinity School, Yale University. Used by permission.

am a reminder of a Christian's obligation to give back to God a portion of His own.

I am a reminder that a church can only exist by the stewardship of its members. I give each member and friend of the church an opportunity to examine his Christian conscience. In a way I'm like Jesus was with Pilate. You have to do *something* with me.

Some people do what Pilate tried to do with Jesus. They drop me in the waste basket—wash their hands of me. They push their own responsibility off on the other members of the church. They are financially able to pledge, but they want the security, the services, the ministry of the church without helping to support it.

Others would like to be able to use me but cannot give. They can return me with a notation to that effect and their prayers and interest thus shown will be a strengthening force even though they have no material means to pledge.

Some people will get me off their hands by filling in a nominal amount. They will pledge two or three dollars a week when they have comfortable homes, automobiles, and luxuries. The two or three dollars for some of these members is just a tip—much less than they spend for many luxuries every week.

Others with substantial incomes will feel better by filling in $5 or $8 or $10. And yet this may represent only 1 or 2 or 3% of their income. I cannot help these people find the true joy of sacrificial giving.

Some members will receive me in true Christian spirit. They see in me an opportunity to express tangibly their love for Christ and His church. Many of these are tithers. They give 10% or more of their income to the church and other religious and charitable causes. They give most of their tithe to the church because it is God's greatest instrument for building the Kingdom.

I am a pledge card—a piece of paper. And yet I am the key to the future of Union Avenue. On Victory Sunday, May 8, I will record the love, the Christian stewardship of a great congregation.

Sincerely,[12]

November 16, 1960

DEAR MEMBER OF IMMANUEL:

Enclosed you will find a pledge card and a copy of the 1961 budget as approved at the last meeting of our congregation. It

[12] Written by John McGinty, Chairman, Budget Underwriting Committee, Union Avenue Christian Church, St. Louis. Used by permission.

is our hope that you will consider the budget, and with thought and prayer fill out the pledge card. The purpose of the pledge card is not to coerce people into giving a certain amount, rather that they may thoughtfully consider their blessings and what they owe to God.

We would remind all, of the responsibilities of a member of the Evangelical and Reformed Church, as found in the Constitution and By-laws of the denomination: Part II, Section 12—"Members of the Church shall live sober, righteous and Godly lives and labor faithfully to bring others to Christ. They shall take an active part in the life and work of the Church. This shall include regular attendance at divine worship; devout use of the Holy Sacraments; diligent observance of private devotions; liberal financial and moral support toward the maintenance of the church and her benevolent undertakings; obedience to her established law and authorities; untiring zeal in bringing the unchurched under her influence; and sincere endeavor to apply the teaching of Jesus to all human relationships. Parents shall provide adequate Christian training for their entire household."

Sometime during the next two weeks, a man from the church will stop at your home. Please have the pledge card ready in a sealed envelope. He will have your envelopes, and be happy to answer any questions concerning the church budget.

We thank you for your cooperation in this matter.

Yours in Christ,[13]

Special Concerns

DEAR MR. _____:

Your mother was a marvelous person and a faithful Christian. She loved _____ Church and supported it in every possible way. She will long be remembered in our congregation and in our lives. Persons like Mrs. _____ build great traditions, institutions and common faith.

In the past few years, we have had an increasing number of our deceased members memorialized by their families. This is a permanent way of perpetuating their memory and their influence. Thinking that you and your sisters would be interested in such an expression of love, I make bold to mention a few things which we need at the church and which would be suitable memorials.

AIR CONDITIONING: While there may be some who consider

[13] Written by Robert Utke, Pastor, Evangelical and Reformed Church, Milwaukee. Used by permission.

church air conditioning a luxury, apparently it is not so considered by business. There are many people who would find it most difficult living without it in the summer months. Like your mother, many of our older members cannot come to church during the heat of the summer and especially knowing the building will be uncomfortable. A few years ago, we had a survey of our needs in this area. To air condition the entire church was estimated to run from $50,000 to $60,000. We could not afford it. Since then, we have air conditioned all of our offices and a number of our class rooms for small children. A substantial gift would enable us to realize more of our ultimate needs in this area.

GOLDEN AGE GROUP: Like all metropolitan churches, we have a great number of members who are in their seventies and eighties. A few years ago we started a weekday program for these, our senior citizens, called the Golden Age Club. They come to the church and/or are brought on given days for an interesting program and fellowship. Mrs. _____ thoroughly enjoyed it. The number in this group will be increasing. If this work could be endowed in an amount that would yield us from $400 to $500 annually, it would enable us to do more for this important and frequently neglected age group. It could bear the name of your mother.

EXTERIOR LIGHTING: Because of the location of our church, as well as enhancing its beauty by night, there are those who feel that the exterior of our building should be well illuminated. This possibility was explored some time ago and the estimates ran from $2,000 to $2,500.

CONCERT PIANO: We need a concert piano to replace one that is beyond satisfactory and reasonable repair. We are advised that a Steinway concert grand will run from $6,000 to $7,200, less 15% for a church.

Knowing of Mrs. _____'s desire to do something in the way of a sizeable capital investment in the future of our church, I hope that you may find it in your heart to take up the matter with your sisters and establish a worthy memorial to your mother in _____ Church.

With appreciation for your consideration, and with all good wishes, I am

Sincerely,

DEAR MR. _____:

Inasmuch as I shall be leaving the city tomorrow and the country Friday, and knowing all too well that something could happen to either one or both of us before we meet again, I am taking this means of laying a concern upon your heart.

_____, you are one of the very few members left in our congregation whom the Lord has blessed with material gains, far in excess of the average person, and to whom I can now turn. Those of us who know the church, appreciate your support and loyalty through the years.

My present concern is the condition of our pipe organ. According to information, the men who re-worked the instrument fulfilled their contract and did a good job so far as they went. Enough was not done. The organ needs considerable work. Some even question if it can be satisfactorily completed. Moreover, nothing has been spent on it since it was installed. Were it not for the fact that we have an exceptional organist, we would have had more difficulty. He is very discouraged about it.

At this juncture, no one knows what it would cost to complete the refinements necessary. We may be able to get by for $20,000 or it may run $30,000. Whatever the final cost, it will still be lower than the price of a new organ of comparable size and tone. Much time has been invested in exploring the situation and the study continues.

_____, I wish you would accept the organ as your project, assume the cost of final completion of the instrument, which is capable of being a superior one, and then permit the church to dedicate it to the memory of your _____, whom, I am told, loved stately music and wanted to see the church have a better organ. I pray that you may find it in your heart to accept this challenge and to invest in the future of _____.

In the introduction to *The Spiritual Legacy of John Foster Dulles,* Dr. Henry P. Van Dusen, President of Union Theological Seminary, New York City, reminds us of the character and faith of the late Secretary of State. Mr. Dulles loved the church and faithfully served it. He loved church music. "It was no accident that, in his last days, when suffering sharpened and the inescapable end threatened, he longed to hear again the hymns that had nourished his spirit in youth and across the years. . . ." A number of fine recordings of hymns were provided, among them his favorites: "The Spacious Firmament on High;" "God of Our Life, Through All the Circling Years;" "Work for the Night is Coming." Dr. Van Dusen continues by saying, "And so . . . night by night, the waning spirit was rekindled by the great hymns of Christian faith." John Foster Dulles died to the music of the church.

There is but one privilege greater than hearing church music —providing it. What a privilege to be able to provide a church and one's own heart with the hymns of faith.

Thanking you for considering this permanent ministry, I am
Gratefully and sincerely,

American Colony Jerusalem

December, 1960

DEAR FRIEND:

One of the great personalities of our time is that most remarkable woman, well known to you, Mrs. Bertha Spafford Vester of Jerusalem. The great men of Middle East history from the days of Lawrence of Arabia, Lord Allenby, Sir John Simons, Lord Balfour and King Hussein—all have held her in admiration, and today she is perhaps the most beloved figure in the Holy Land.

But her chief claim upon our high regard and affection lies in her dedicated human service. Those of you who have visited the Holy Land will recall the wide incidence of sickness and suffering, especially among the children of the poor. And there are lots of poor and lots of children. These youngsters are as appealing as children anywhere in the world. And the suffering among them from undernourishment and disease has touched the hearts of all who have seen these lovable boys and girls of the Holy City.

Mrs. Vester is really doing something about these needy children. Mothers by the hundreds bring little ones with big wonder-filled eyes to Mrs. Vester's children's hospital. There they are given medical attention by the two doctors on the staff, the Doctors Dajani, who are as effective physicians as I have ever watched at work. They seem to have some healing magic in their touch that sends these youngsters out well and happy. If you were to walk through the hospital with Mrs. Vester and the doctors and see the gratitude written on the faces of the children, you would never forget it.

Wouldn't you like to join with me in helping Mrs. Vester in her dedicated work for children of the Holy Land? We want to raise a sizeable fund at this Christmas season, for the hospital is in desperate need of funds. Also, in helping this work you will strengthen friendship for America in a part of the world where we too need friends.

Here is a gift from which you can take a lot of satisfaction.

You can give by check or stock certificate made payable to the American Colony Charities Association. Of course your gift is tax deductible. For your convenience I enclose a card and self-addressed envelope.

I expect very soon to pay another visit to Mrs. Vester's children's hospital inside the ancient walls of Old Jerusalem. I know how happy she will be when I bring your generous gifts to her. I hope to hear from you soon.

Cordially yours,[14]

SEASONAL

Holy days and holidays afford opportunities to communicate the message of the church. Here again, one needs to be careful lest seasonal messages become perfunctory. Through his letters the minister has the singular privilege of preparing his people for Christian participation in the high days of the church.

Lent

February 24, 1960

DEAR FRIEND:

I take this special opportunity to visit with you by means of this letter as the Lenten season draws near. I hope you will feel the need of spiritual renewal as well as the special need of coming to God's house for worship.

During this season, we want to concentrate on the meaning of the cross. What finer beginning could we find than in the celebration of the Holy Communion. Thus we will have a communion service on Ash Wednesday evening at 8:00. All of our Wednesday evening services will begin at 8:00 P.M. Wednesday evening and Sunday morning worship services will all follow the same theme.

During the Lenten season each year our Churches join with other Churches all over the world in the observance of The One Great Hour of Sharing. The day for which this has been planned this year is Sunday, March 27th. You will receive more information later.

[14] Written by Lowell Thomas, Rockefeller Center, New York. Used by permission.

Wednesday evening March 9th the Pastor's Aid will lead us in their annual Lenten Quiet Hour Service. Even though the ladies will be in charge of this service it is still a very important part of our worship. It is good when our own folk can lead us in our worship of God.

The Council is again providing Lenten envelopes for your convenience. They hope that these will be of help to you as you lay aside each week that which you intend for God. You will find these enclosed in this letter. By vote of the Congregation this money will be used for our Apportionment.

So as this season comes closer and as we attempt to look at the Cross from several directions may our hearts and souls be lifted to God. May God Bless you.

Sincerely,[15]

Thanksgiving

November 23, 1960

DEAR BLESSED FRIEND:

How can any thinking person give thanks in the midst of the problems of our present age? The answer is found in the Bible, for it is filled with thanksgiving by people fully aware of the perils of their times. Daniel, threatened with death, faces his windows toward Jerusalem, praising God. The Psalmist recites the evils of his age, the dangers which beset him, yet continually breaks into praises to Jehovah. Paul and Silas, in prison sing praises to God. Our Lord, on the night He is betrayed takes bread and breaks it and gives thanks.

The Pilgrims, with the Bible in their hands and hearts, observed the first American Thanksgiving in sight of the rounded graves of more than half their company. They had borne great hardship because of their faith and the end of their suffering was not in sight. Amid the anguish of the Civil War, Abraham Lincoln, nurtured on the Bible, proclaimed a Day of Thanksgiving. It became an annual observance.

Only the Bible can show us how to face reality and still give thanks. If we wait until our family is in perfect health and we have no sorrow, no troubles, and no anxieties, we will never give thanks. But our faith is rooted in a Cross; and we give thanks—

[15] Written by Dwayne Dollgener, Pastor, St. Peters United Church of Christ, Evangelical and Reformed, Coupland, Texas. Used by permission.

in the midst of personal difficulties and seemingly insurmountable national and international problems. We can be fully aware of the dangers and evils about us and, at the same time, lay hold of the promise—"In everything by prayer and supplication, with thanksgiving, let your requests be made known unto God, and the peace of God, which passeth all understanding, shall keep your hearts and minds through Christ Jesus."

Our 1960 Thanksgiving is remarkably similar to that of Paul, who stood on a storm-tossed ship which had not been able to chart a course for fourteen days and fourteen nights, and who, in complete awareness of threatened destruction, "took bread and gave thanks to God in the presence of them."

The result of that Thanksgiving was such confidence and action by passengers and crew alike that they all reached shore safely. There are many of our day who believe our ship is off any course ever charted by God or man, and that for many long days we have not seen the sun of wisdom, the moon of mercy or the stars of hope. If we of Third Baptist Church will let the Holy Spirit speak to us through the Bible and continue to share the Good News with all the world, that Jesus died for sinners, we have reason to hope that many who are now in despair will be of good cheer, and we, too, will come through the storm that threatens our age.

Your devoted pastor,[16]

Christmas

December 23, 1960

DEAR _____ :

The Gospel of Luke reminds us that on the night the infant Jesus was born Joseph and Mary found refuge in a Bethlehem stable because "there was no place for them in the inn."

There is something strangely prophetic about these words in Luke's narrative. Just as there was no place for the Babe of Bethlehem in the inn, so there has been little place for Christ and his teachings in the hearts of men down through the years. There are many who give nominal allegiance to Christ as Lord, but how many really make a place for him and his ways in their daily lives?

[16] Written by Dr. Sterling L. Price, Minister, Third Baptist Church, St. Louis. Used by permission.

As we prepare to celebrate another anniversary of the birth of our Lord, we would do well to face seriously the question, "Wherein are we failing to make a place for him who is the Lord of life?" At this season of the year, when we recall the birth of our Lord, it is also well that we think of those of our fellows in various parts of our world who have been denied places worthy of their dignity as human beings and as children of God. For example:

The natives of Southwest Africa, who as wards of a white dominated state—the Union of South Africa—have a status little better than the serfs of the Middle Ages. . . . The Jews of Europe who survived the brutalities of Hitler's regime, many of whom still feel like aliens in an unfriendly society. . . . The hundreds of thousands of refugees throughout the world who have little hope for their or their children's future. . . . The negroes in our own land, where the Christian Church has been so long dominant, who are struggling for a place as first-class citizens which has thus far been denied them. . . . The Christians in East Germany who are being systematically deprived of basic freedoms by an all-powerful communist state.

This list can be extended indefinitely, but it is evident that those of us who are concerned about Christian education in an unchristian world have many unfinished tasks facing us at home and abroad. To you who share the important responsibility our Board is called upon to carry out in these times, I extend grateful thanks for the loyalty and devotion you have shown throughout the year.

May the Lord whose birth we celebrate at Christmas grant you and yours all that is good in this holiday season and in the New Year ahead.

Cordially yours,[17]

[17] Written by F. I. Sheeder, Executive Secretary, United Church of Christ, Evangelical and Reformed Church, Philadelphia. Used by permission.

5

Within the Church Family

The correspondence within the congregation is a demanding yet significant ministry. When properly conceived and timed, letters will do much to promote program, good will, and genuine fellowship. It is a common tendency of us all to overlook those immediately associated with us in our work, for we assume that they will know the calendar and special occasions as well as our own feelings. Consequently we often fail to communicate with them. The larger the parish and community the more imperative are written communications. Whoever is responsible for the calendar of the church should not permit the administrator or minister to forget the many occasions which require a letter to some group, class, or individual within the fellowship of the church.

SIGNIFICANT EVENTS

Whereas every event is significant if it is worthy of the sponsorship of the church, some by nature demand more promotion and spiritual preparation than others. A letter not only announces and promotes the occasion but also interprets purpose and possibilities and projects hopes. Indeed every aspect of church life might well benefit and be enriched by thoughtful correspondence.

Catechetical Class

DEAR ONES IN CHRIST:

Greetings in the blessed name of our Lord Jesus! Our hearts do rejoice because so many families are taking such a deep interest in the catechetical program of our church. This instruction was resumed last week for the children between the ages 8 and 16 with 88 pupils in attendance. Others have enrolled since. The vast majority of our church families have enrolled their children this year. We want to believe that you too want to send your children and thus be numbered among those who diligently instruct their children in God's word of salvation. (Deuteronomy 6:7).

Many of us, by God's grace, have entered into covenant with our Lord when we presented our children for baptism. What a blessed day that was when we claimed that covenant for our child and we promised the Lord to instruct that child in His Word to the utmost of our power, in order that that child might be truly His. And we want to keep that vow with all sacred regard for we know that His blessings are conditioned on our keeping that vow. "Pay thy vows unto the Most High: and call upon me in the day of trouble: I will deliver thee, and thou shalt glorify me." (Psalm 50:14–15). If we keep our vows, He will hear our prayers in behalf of our children. Oh, how much they need our prayers in this day! And if we have not yet so entered into covenant with the Lord, may the day soon come that we shall be led to do so.

We do anticipate seeing your child (children) at the next meeting of the catechism classes.

Yours in Christ Jesus,[1]

Though approaches might differ, certainly this pastor is voicing joy at the prospect of a large membership class. He is also citing the place of children in the family of the church and the responsibility of parents to see that this is accomplished.

BUILDING BOOM

We are witnessing an unprecedented boom in church building. The United States Census Bureau reports that for 1960 church build-

[1] Written by Frank Snuttjer, Minister, Salem Reformed Church, Little Rock, Iowa. Used by permission.

ing topped one billion dollars for the first time, despite a so-called recession. Seventy-three million is listed for December, 1960, alone. The volume of church construction has doubled since 1954. We should hope that spiritual progress has paralleled facility improvement and expansion. The minister must constantly challenge his people to be increasingly worthy stewards of their abilities and resources.

DEAR FRIENDS:

It has been a little less than three years since our church moved to Clayton and McKnight Roads! We are completing the second phase of our Building Program and will move into our beautiful new sanctuary within the next few months.

This progress represents careful planning, hard work, prayer, and generous giving by the majority of our membership. It is thrilling to realize how widespread the interest and support have been. We have undertaken a Building Program which has made challenging demands upon us. Without your sacrificial giving, we could not have attained our present goal. A big job is yet before us in completing the work we have begun.

We must provide a building with facilities that are needed for a program of worship, Christian education, and service adequate to the demands of an exacting and difficult period of history in the world. If this is to be done, each of us must do his best to give to the fullest extent of our resources. No person could ask for more devoted people with whom to work.

Faithfully yours,[2]

This is a warm and friendly message of gratitude and challenge.

Regular Attendance

One of America's ablest preachers once remarked that Sunday worship in the church he served was always "an event." It should be so in every church. However, we know how easy it is to take for granted the needs of people. The dynamic church will be a church involved with people, constantly seeking to confront them with the claims of Jesus. Christians need to be reminded again and again that the *great commission* is personal. It is important for pro-

---

[2] Written by Dr. Leon R. Robison, Jr., Minister, Second Baptist Church, St. Louis. Used by permission.

fessing Christians to realize that no church worthy of the name is local. By its very design and concept the church is universal.

DEAR FRIEND:

Each of us wants to do something about conditions today. But what can you do, beyond thinking, talking, and praying?

One thing is to reach out for people and bring them into our dynamic spiritual fellowship at Marble Collegiate Church. As we add numbers and dedication to Christ's church, we shall be adding to spiritual forces in human affairs.

The enclosed card has been prepared in the hope that our members will use it to invite friends and neighbors to the church. Additional cards may be found on the sermon racks at the church entrances. Why not place them judiciously among neighbors in your apartment house? Perhaps you will give them to fellow-workers in your office and mail them to your friends.

Also, arrange to meet those whom you invite and introduce them to the ministers and to other members. Especially give names and addresses to the Reverend Eugene M. Pierce.

There are thousands of unchurched people in New York City. Let us go out for them and bring them into Marble Church. This is a constructive way to help build a better world.

Thank you for your fine cooperation. It will be very helpful.

Cordially,[3]

One can feel the personality and passion of Norman Vincent Peale in this compelling letter. He provides everyone with a share of this vital Christian task.

Disciplinary Letter

There was a time when this type of letter was more commonly used than now. However, it has its place. Church membership is a serious business.

DEAR FRIEND:

The Spiritual Committee met last evening to study the roll of our Church relative to our annual report to the Denomination to be made next month.

Because of the apportionment we pay to the Denomination

[3] Written by Dr. Norman Vincent Peale, Minister, Marble Collegiate Church, New York. Used by permission.

for each member, it is important that we keep only active members on our roll. The requirements for active membership are rather elementary: 1: Attendance at worship services as often as possible 2: Observance of Holy Communion of record at least once a year and 3: A contribution of record at least once a year.

Inasmuch as you are delinquent on all three counts, you leave us no alternative but to erase your name from our rolls at the end of the year. Membership in the Church of Jesus Christ is a highly important matter, and should not be regarded lightly.

We should be delighted to have you restore your good standing by visiting with us at the next communion service on December 4th, thus communing and contributing of record. Or if you wish, we would be glad to send your letter of transfer to the Church you are now attending.

We covet your continued interest in the work of the church, which is the cause of Christ. We shall be delighted to learn of your renewed interest before the end of the year.

Sincerely yours,[4]

While few of us would have the temerity to use this frank letter, many would admire such courage. In some communions a letter of this nature would emanate from a lay official.

BETWEEN CHURCH OFFICIALS

Consecrated officers of the church are involved in a heavy flow of correspondence with one another in the performance of their responsibilities. The more functional the organization and the more people involved, the greater the necessity for officers to use written communications.

Budget Preparation

SUBJECT: Proposed 1960–61 Budget to be presented to Board and Congregation on Wednesday evening, March 9, immediately following Fellowship Dinner Meeting.
ENCLOSURE: Proposed 1959–60 Budget

[4] Written by Jesse Deardorff, Pastor, Protestant Community Church (United Church of Christ), Baltimore. Used by permission.

DEAR FRIENDS:

1. In accordance with the direction of the Personnel and Policy Committee (Mr. _____, Chairman) and prior discussion of February 28, 1960, with Mr. Claude L. Welch, we are pleased to attach hereto the work sheet or pages pertaining to your individual department (or departments) and covering the proposed budget, which is to be submitted to the Board-Congregation on the evening of March 9 immediately following the Fellowship Meeting.

2. Just prior to the Board Meeting, we will pass out to all church members in attendance a summary of the proposed budget giving the individual totals by departments and the grand total, which is $135,686 as shown on the attached summary work sheet.

3. Questions will be invited from those in attendance and if a question should concern a particular department, your Chairman plans on calling each department to answer that question. Therefore, please be in attendance and with your Committee be prepared to answer these questions.

4. Mr. Welch advanced the opinion that the proposed budget represents a "sensible" challenge. This proposed budget takes into consideration a modest 2% increase over last year's budget. It also includes extra fire insurance on our building, the premium of which comes due in this coming fiscal year. Further, the new proposed budget includes additional for postage and printing. All of these extra items can be well substantiated as we well know, and again Union Avenue has a realistic and a sound challenge ahead for all of us.

Sincerely,[5]

Everyone can perform more effectively when he receives such a clear and factual message.

Policy and Personnel Committee

To: *Policy and Personnel Committee*

DEAR _____:

I think that in the very near future the Policy and Personnel Committee should have a meeting to consider:

[5] Written by Carl F. Gast, Chairman, Budget Preparation Committee, Union Avenue Christian Church, St. Louis. Used by permission.

1. Manner in which we should honor Mrs. —————.
2. Manner in which we should use money from Mr. —————.
Dr. Jones and I would like to meet with you on these matters. If you care to invite them, the three vice-presidents might also like to meet with us.

Sincerely,[6]

Though friendly and informal, this is a very businesslike letter.

Functional Organization

July 10, 1959

Dear Shepherds:

The Membership Care assignments for 1959–60 have been mailed to our Elders and Deacons. Their responsibility for the care and development of the congregation replaces that formerly assigned to you as shepherds.

I want to take this opportunity to thank you for the service which you have rendered under the Shepherding Program. I speak in behalf of the staff, the board and the Membership Department as well as myself.

Some men who have served as shepherds will also receive new Membership Care assignments, because as Deacons they will automatically become Group Leaders in the new program.

Sincerely,[7]

WELCOME

The church office, whether that of a multiple ministry or a single person, should be alert to the propitiousness and importance of letters of welcome. These range from greetings to new neighbors in the community, newcomers to worship, and new members in the church to those appointed to places of leadership within the congregation. This intimate, warm overture of friendship and cordiality not only strengthens public relations throughout the com-

[6] Written by Mrs. Carl F. Gast, President, Official Board, Union Avenue Christian Church, St. Louis. Used by permission.

[7] Written by James L. Pennington, Assistant Minister, Union Avenue Christian Church, St. Louis. Used by permission.

munity but also immeasurably contributes to the sense of belonging within the congregation.

New Neighbors

DEAR _____:

Welcome! We hope you are enjoying living in _____ and that you felt at home worshipping with us.

I wish my schedule permitted me to call on each new family personally, but it simply is not possible. However, someone from our Board of Deacons will contact you shortly and will want to get acquainted with you personally and tell you about our church.

Perhaps you would like to receive our weekly newsletter, "Wood Chips." If so, just call the church office (MI 7-2550) and Mrs. _____, the church secretary, will add your name to our mailing list.

Please do not hesitate to call upon us if there is some further way in which we may be of help to you.

Yours very truly,[8]

To a Visitor

Thank you for telling us you worshipped with us last Sunday. It inspires us to know that fellow-Christians from other Churches worship with us from time to time.

If ever we may be of service to you, please call on us. God bless you richly.

Sincerely yours,[9]

New Member

A letter of welcome from the minister of the church to one who has committed himself to work and witness for Christ is a marvelous privilege. Though a flexible, personalized form letter may be developed, it should be informal and communicate the personal interest of the minister and the affection of the people.

[8] Written by Bernard R. Hawley, Pastor, The Woods Memorial Presbyterian Church, Severna Park, Maryland. Used by permission.

[9] Written by Dr. David A. MacLennan, Minister, The Brick Presbyterian Church, Rochester, New York. Used by permission.

DEAR _____ :

We cordially welcome you into our Church, to this intimate association with us, and to the privileges which we enjoy. We promise you our affection and care and pray that our united efforts may be fruitful in the work of the Kingdom.

Church membership, rightly valued, is a badge of distinction to be worn with dignity and honor. The Church member is a certain kind of person who stands before the world for things of righteousness, and who gives evidence of high purpose and moral courage. The world needs that kind of living now.

May I remind you of the importance of your religious duties and privileges in the midst of the pressure and pull of life. Regular church attendance, the use of personal prayer, and the devotional study of the Bible are essential to a happy religious experience. Take a regular part in the work of the Church and invite others to work with you. Above all things, be loyal to Christ and to Central Church.

May God help you to be faithful in every inward thought and outward deed.

One of our modern poets has changed a few words of Alan Seeger's famous poem. The idea he conveys represents an excellent ideal of each of us.

> I have a rendezvous with Christ,
> And if I to my pledgèd word am true,
> I shall not fail that rendezvous.

Cordially yours,[10]

DEAR _____ :

This is to tell you what a joy it was to have you become a part of Community Christian Church.

The privileges and responsibilities of discipleship are many, and let me urge you to share in both and thus make your Church membership with us count for great things as we go forward together. Our church, like all true churches of our Lord, is a comradeship of love and service. Our fellowship comes from that heartwarming sense of spiritual oneness held by us all because of the things we share in common. You and I are indeed fortunate to be a part of such a fellowship and let us bear witness to its excellence in every possible way.

[10] Written by Dr. Frederick H. Olert, Minister, Central Presbyterian Church, Kansas City, Missouri. Used by permission.

If there is any service I can render you at any time, please do not fail to call upon me.

Accept me always as,

Your friend and brother,[11]

New Baby

DEAR _____:

So you have finally arrived in this big old world! We are so happy that you have come to take your place in that grand [name of family] with [name of children, if any]. They have planned with great anticipation for your coming, and you are fortunate indeed to have such a fine Christian home!

I covet for you the experience you will have under the influence of Christian parents. During the early years they will train you up in the way you should go, and as you come to that period of adolescence which is so important, you will have already built a foundation for your life which will prove most helpful. The years ahead will be interesting and happy ones.

The Church will hold an important place in your life, and I want you to remember through all of your life that in the teachings of Jesus we find the only basis for complete living. I pray God's richest blessing on you as you grow in wisdom and in stature. May the days of your years be fruitful ones in service and in love for your family, your nation and your Father God.

Very sincerely,

Your first pastor [12]

CHURCH OFFICERS

Anyone accepting leadership in the church appreciates a letter of welcome. Here the timing is extremely important, and the letter should reflect confidence.

DEAR _____:

In selecting you to become a member of the Official Family of Union Avenue Christian Church, our Nominating Committee

[11] Written by Dr. Frank Johnson Pippin, Minister, The Community Christian Church, Kansas City, Missouri. Used by permission.

[12] Written by Dr. Myron C. Cole, Hollywood-Beverly Christian Church, Los Angeles. Used by permission.

based its consideration and decision on a number of your personal qualifications; especially your interest in the total Church program.

Next Wednesday evening's dinner, May 8, at 6:30 will be followed by one of the most important Church meetings of the year.

New and present members of the Official Family will have an opportunity to become better acquainted with each other, and to learn of plans pointing to the continued growth and development of Union Avenue.

We trust you will make a special effort to be present.

Sincerely,[13]

CHURCH SCHOOL CORRESPONDENCE

The Sunday Church School is the lifeblood of the church. Irrespective of the number and caliber of staff personnel, correspondence with the working corps of the Sunday School is essential to effective communication. Not only do the personnel need encouragement, but at times they need to be reminded of their mission, namely, to witness for Christ and the whole church. It is all too easy for a class to become an isolated unit within the fellowship.

Concerning Cooperation

DEAR TEACHERS AND PRESIDENTS:

I have just been looking again at the tape measure provided us by our Ways and Means Committee where we can see how each of our Organized Classes and Departments gave to our budget last year.

However, we must not be at ease in Zion and to that end I am adjuring you with all the earnestness of my heart to see that the members of your class who have not turned their pledge cards in by Sunday, November 13th, or who have not given their word that they will pledge are contacted during the week before Victory Day, November 20th. The success of this campaign depends upon your leadership and ability to have all of these members visited.

[13] Written by Dr. Lin D. Cartwright, Nominating Committee, Union Avenue Christian Church, St. Louis. Used by permission.

Remember this, that if they cannot be present on November 20th, they can either give their pledge card to the one who visits them or they can mail the pledge card to the church office.

We will give you, in this envelope, some extra pledge cards and also some extra envelopes to leave with those who are to make pledges.

We, naturally, expect great things from our Sunday School when we have leaders such as you in key places of responsibility. Our Lord's work waits on your glad response to this challenge.

God love you!

Your devoted pastor,[14]

New Church School Equipment

This letter was sent to all teachers of the Sunday Church School to introduce new equipment and to remind them of stewardship implications.

DEAR FRIENDS:

I am writing you about the new church school equipment that is just beginning to arrive. I believe this is the most important letter that I have ever written you.

This equipment is very good. It is as durable and sturdy as can be purchased. IT IS OUR RESPONSIBILITY, as teachers and parents, to see that the children learn to CARE FOR EACH PIECE. This is how Christian stewardship is practiced and taught, and teaching stewardship is an important part of the Christian Education for children.

These are not "play toys" in the sense that term is usually used. This is equipment planned for the age-level of the child to provide experiences for his development as God would have him to grow. Through their use his religious life may be greatly enriched.

Many times you, as a teacher or adult helper, will need to *set limits* with the children as they use this equipment. Perhaps this can best be done through conversation in a "together time." Sometimes you, as an adult, may need to be very firm and your decision may not be what the child wants to do. Speak to him kindly but firmly but with respect and appreciation for him as a person. With threes, fours, and fives, a simple explanation as to

[14] Written by Dr. Sterling L. Price, Minister, Third Baptist Church, St. Louis. Used by permission.

"why" will help him to accept your decision in a much finer spirit. THIS IS YOUR ROLE.

Too, this is the way learning takes place. It is the only way children can have a learning, growing experience and be happy in a large group of children. Children have a right to know what is expected of them and to be able to depend upon the adults guiding them to help them live up to what is expected of them. Only then can they feel secure in the situation in which they find themselves. THIS IS CHRISTIAN NURTURE.

These are the children's rooms. The children must be shown their responsibility for putting away their equipment, caring for it at all times (washing tables off after pasting) and leaving their rooms in order BEFORE THEY GO HOME. It is the adults' responsibility to see that this is done by working with the children.

This we know—the children will appreciate and enjoy their church to the extent they are helped to do these things. May God bless you and enrich your lives as you give of yourselves in this very important work of the church.

Your co-worker and friend,[15]

New Baby

DEAR MOM:

Am I keeping you away from Church? Or am I imagining things? I heard you saying to Pop last Sunday that you'd surely like to get to a Church Service once in a while but what would you do with me.

Besides being your latest "Income-Tax-Exemption," I know that I am somewhat of a nuisance at times. But, Mom, you know how much I love you. You know that I will kick and scream if you so much as try to slip out that door, and leave me with one of those baby sitters. *But,* now things have changed! Believe it or not, I have a new viewpoint on life. Honest I have! And this is how it came about.

I learned (oh, a little bird told me) that the Park Avenue Christian Church had made special arrangements to take care of us future deacons and deaconesses by enlarging their Nursery space. More bed space has been provided also. And for those of us who can move about there is a large pen. (Of course, there may be a fist fight or two in the pen, but our muscles must de-

[15] Written by Mrs. W. R. Watkins, Director, Children's Work and Family Life, Union Avenue Christian Church, St. Louis. Used by permission.

velop, you know.) There are some of us who can be trusted outside that pen, so there are some grand toys to play with. Also, a lovely Red Box that gives out the loveliest music—those Nursery Rhymes which I like.

For those who are "going on 3" there is a class. Yes, indeed, a *Class!* You'd be surprised how much these boys and girls can learn. There are songs, stories and a time to be quiet and think about God. Last Sunday, some of the children could be heard singing "Jesus Loves Me" (that little bird again!).

You and Pop both need a time in the week to sit still and be quiet and listen to God's message. You can do this while I am in Church School. Isn't it wonderful that the Park Avenue Christian Church has provided this lovely arrangement for all of us?

Please, Mom—and Pop, too—think it over. I want to go to Church, and I want you both to go too! Come on, huh?

Love and kisses from your devoted
JUNIOR AND JUNIOR MISS [16]

The above letter with a picture of an infant in the left-hand corner was very captivating. It would certainly give "Mother and Dad" qualms of conscience if they did not attend church with their child.

FELLOWSHIP GROUPS AND DEPARTMENTS

In addition to Sunday Church School classes there are many groups, auxiliaries, and departments within the fellowship of the church that need staff direction and coordination. Thoughtful letters are indispensable in creating and maintaining an effective organization.

Evangelism

New Member Calling

DEAR FRIENDS:

Many thanks again to you who have heretofore helped to attain our GOAL OF 200 NEW MEMBERS by _____ [date], by calling one or two new member prospects within a one week period.

[16] Written by Department of Christian Education, Park Avenue Christian Church, New York. Used by permission.

The results of your calls are encouraging and necessitate a monthly repetition of our calling-within-a-week basis on our growing list of prospective members, now large enough for everyone being assigned names of one or two of such prospects.

Therefore, our _____ [month] PROSPECT CALLING will again be at the callers' discretion.

DURING THE ONE WEEK PERIOD commencing _____ [date] and ending _____ [date] and bringing or mailing the results of such calls to the church on or before _____ [date].

All callers will please pick up their visitation Assignments in _____ office immediately after the Sunday morning service on _____ [date].

Please fill out the enclosed form and mail or deliver it to the church as therein shown.

With sincere thanks,[17]

An attempt to keep the fires burning!

Membership Development

DEAR _____:

Have you found time and made the effort to call upon the families assigned to you for the cultivation of more intensive Christian fellowship in our church? If you have, your experiences have probably varied. You have found happiness and occasionally some sorrow. You have at times been depressed but also you have been lifted up.

At your earliest convenience please complete your first "get acquainted calls" and make a report to your Division Elder.

While you have been calling _____, our faithful administrative assistants have been checking on church attendance for us. The enclosed report indicates how faithful our members have been during the 14 week period _____ – _____ [dates] inclusive. Our Assistant Minister, _____, has reviewed these reports and has recommended that personal calls be made promptly on certain members.

Sunday church service attendance at _____ [name of church] followed by our friendly fellowship hour should become

[17] By Roy B. Hansen, Chairman, Cultivation Committee, Department of Evangelism, and Randolph H. Weber, Chairman, Department of Evangelism, Union Avenue Christian Church, St. Louis. Used by permission.

a habit with all members. The rich rewards from regular attendance can be attested to best by loyal members like yourself. Won't you please make the recommended calls at once urging church attendance during the weeks ahead? Be regular in attendance yourself and look for those you have called.

Please fill out and return the Visitation reports to your Division Elder who will turn them in to Mr. _____ in the Membership Office. The results will be properly recorded on the Membership records.

May Our Lord richly reward you for this service.

Sincerely yours,[18]

This is a needling letter.

INTERSTAFF COMMUNICATIONS

In addition to staff conferences, the minister must keep every member of the staff aware of program changes and pending developments. In like manner, the staff members should keep him advised. The temptation is to communicate verbally rather than to transmit in writing information, directives, or assignments. Helpful forms may be created to expedite interstaff communications.

One of the time-consuming tasks in a sizable church is that of receiving and channeling telephone calls. The person answering the telephone on a given day should be provided with a simple printed pad to record and to forward messages to staff members not available when the call is received. See form, top of page 80.

Each member of the staff should be provided with a pad about 5½-by-8 inches in color, preferably with the name of the church at the top, staff members appropriately listed.

See form, bottom of page 80.

The orginator of the message should be responsible for its distribution to the staff members. If it is an emergency, it should be delivered personally at once. If not, it should be placed in the staff member's mailbox or on his desk.

[18] Written by Lawrence E. Smith, Chairman, Department of Membership, Union Avenue Christian Church, St. Louis. Used by permission.

NAME OF CHURCH

To _____

Date _____ Time _____

While you were out

Mr. _____

of _____

Phone _____

Telephoned.   Please call him.

Returned your call.   Will call again.

Wants to see you.   Rush.

MESSAGE _____

_____

NAME OF CHURCH

ADDRESS

STAFF COMMUNICATION

TO: Minister   Assistant Minister

       Minister to Youth   Business Administrator

       Children's Worker   Minister of Music

                               Secretaries

Others _____

From _____ Date _____

Subject _____

CALLING REPORTS

Those responsible for parish calling, be they ministers or lay workers, should have a systematic method of recording various types of visits.

NAME OF CHURCH
ADDRESS

Attention: _____

CALLING REPORT

Name _____

Address _____

Member _____ Prospect _____

Special Concern _____

Hospitalized at _____

Could Work in _____

Date _____ Caller _____

See remarks on reverse side.

Summary calling slips are important to the administrator or minister in charge. The form at the top of the next page is a sample of such a report.

```
┌─────────────────────────────────────────────────────────┐
│                     NAME OF CHURCH                        │
│                                                           │
│               CONSOLIDATED CALLING REPORT                 │
│                                                           │
│   Period covered:                                         │
│      Month of _____    │
│      Week of _____    │
│                                                           │
│   Summary of calls:                                       │
│      Prospect Calls          _____     │
│      Pastoral Calls          _____     │
│      Hospital Calls          _____     │
│      Total for the period    _____     │
│                                                           │
│                                                           │
│   Caller _____        │
│   Date Submitted _____        │
│                                                           │
└─────────────────────────────────────────────────────────┘
```

ILLNESS AND DEATH

The church fulfills a never-to-be-forgotten ministry when it communicates news of illness and tragedy to its staff and members quickly and accurately. Emergencies have a way of frustrating people, and they assume that others know of a tragedy simply because they do. It is most helpful to develop an information sheet in the church office which can be filled in by the person who first receives the message. This person will then distribute the information.

Some find it helpful to associate forms with different colors for various emergencies, thus when a particular sheet is handed to a staff member or left at his desk, he reacts immediately. For example, yellow for serious illness, green for report of marriage, pink for membership termination.

Following are some illustrations [19]:

[19] The following forms were developed under the direction of James L. Pennington, Assistant Minister, in cooperation with other staff members of Union Avenue Christian Church, St. Louis.

REPORT OF SERIOUS ILLNESS OR TRAGEDY

STAFF DISTRIBUTION: *Notifications:*

_____Minister   (For Membership Office **only**)

_____Business Office   _____Board Chairman

_____Education Office   _____Shepherding Group

_____Membership Office *FILE*   Person notified:_____

_____Ch. Sch. Class **Pres.**

(If initiated by an office other than the Membership Office, please initial the actions you have taken.)

Person notified:_____

_____CWF, CMF, or C.W.

Person notified:_____

Name _____

Address _____

Church Membership Status _____

Relatives in Union Avenue _____

Became ill or was injured: Date_____ Hour_____

_____Is in the_____Hospital

Address _____

_____Is at home at the home address given above.

_____Is at the home of_____

Address _____

Visitors: None_____Family Only_____Anybody_____

Date of Report_____

Person who contacted the Staff: Name_____

Phone _____

REPORT OF DEATH AND FUNERAL ARRANGEMENTS

STAFF DISTRIBUTION:

_____Minister

_____Education Office

_____Business Office

_____Membership Office *FILE*

(If initiated by an office other than the Membership Office, please initial the action you have taken.)

Notifications:

(For Membership Office Only)

_____Board Chairman

_____Shepherding Group

Person notified:_____

_____Ch. Sch. Class Pres.

Person notified:_____

_____CWF, CMF, or C.W.

Person notified:_____

Name of Deceased_____

Address _____

Church Membership Status_____

Relatives in Union Avenue_____

Deceased: Date_____ Hour_____

Body will be at the_____Funeral Home

Address _____

Times when friends may visit the family at the funeral home:

Funeral Service at_____

Address _____

Date_____ Hour_____

Burial Arrangements: Cemetery_____

Crematory _____

Date _____ Hour _____

Officiating Clergyman _____

Date of Report_____

Person contacting Staff:_____Phone_____

REPORT OF MARRIAGE

BRIDE:

Name_____Old Phone_____

Old Address_____

Church Membership_____

Occupation _____ Employer_____

Business Address_____Business Phone_____

Will continue to work for the same employer: Yes_____No_____

GROOM:

Name_____Old Phone_____

Old Address_____

Church Membership_____

Occupation _____ Employer_____

Business Address_____Business Phone_____

Will continue to work for the same employer: Yes_____No_____

THE WEDDING:

Place _____

Date _____ Clergyman _____

Witnesses:_____   _____

RESIDENCE AFTER MARRIAGE

New Address_____

Date of Residence in the New Home _____New Phone_____

Source of Information_____

Reported by_____Date of Report_____

BUSINESS OFFICE ONLY: Appropriate Correction on Addressograph:_____

MEMBERSHIP OFFICE ONLY: Changes made in Membership Records: __

REPORT OF NEW MEMBER

RECEIVED BY: Confession_____Otherwise_____Date_____

Name_____Home Phone_____

Home Address _____ Zone _____ City _____

Occupation _____ Birthday _____

Employer _____ Business Phone _____

Business Address _____ Zone _____ City _____

CHURCHES IN WHICH YOU HAVE PREVIOUSLY HELD MEMBERSHIP

Church _____ City _____

_____   _____

POSITIONS YOU HAVE HELD IN OTHER CHURCHES: (Include teaching positions)

_____

SCHOOLS ATTENDED:

School_____Major Field_____

_____   _____

HOBBIES AND SPECIAL INTERESTS:

_____

FRATERNAL ORGANIZATIONS AND HONORS:

_____

INFORMATION ABOUT YOUR FAMILY:

Name of Spouse (if married)_____

Occupation _____ Church Membership _____

Employer _____ Address _____

CHILDREN'S NAMES	BIRTH DATES	CHURCH MEMBERSHIP	ATTEND CHURCH SCHOOL AT
_____	_____	_____	_____
_____	_____	_____	_____
_____	_____	_____	_____

REPORT OF MEMBERSHIP TERMINATION

Name _____

Address at time of termination _____

_____

Last address shown on our membership files_____

_____

KIND OF TERMINATION:

_____Transfer of Membership to:

Church _____

Address _____

_____Deceased:

Date _____

Place _____

_____Membership Termination Upon Written Request:

Date _____

(File the request with the **Member-**
ship Office copy of this report)

Remarks: _____

_____

_____

Source of Information_____

Report By:_____Date of Report_____

_____

BUSINESS OFFICE ONLY: Appropriate Correction of Addressograph: _____

MEMBERSHIP OFFICE ONLY: Changes made in Membership Records __

NAME OF CHURCH

WEEKLY REPORT OF WORK ACCOMPLISHED

Number of pieces of mimeographed material produced _____

Number of envelopes used_____ Stencils cut_____

Church Papers mailed _____ Bulletins _____

Other Work_____

_____

4¢ Postage for church letters_____3¢ postage_____Cards_____

Classes: 4¢ postage_____3¢ postage_____Cards_____

Scouts: 4¢ postage_____3¢ postage_____Cards_____

Time spent on Sermon_____

Committee meetings attended (Church)_____(Outside)_____

Pastoral and personal calls made_____

Pastoral conferences held_____

Speaking engagements (Church)_____(Outside)_____

Weddings Performed_____Funerals_____

New Members added_____

Number of Prospect or Evangelistic Telephone Calls_____

Number Other Telephone Calls: Outgoing_____Incoming_____

Long-distance_____

Hours spent in daily routine_____

Number of Meals served in our church: To our own people _____

Others _____

Other people using the building _____

Amount of time spent in cleaning building_____

Number of daily errands_____

Amount of time spent on grounds of our church_____

My biggest problem this week_____

My suggestions for next week_____

Date _____ Signature _____ Title _____

6

Appreciation and Praise

In their splendid book *The Mind Goes Forth*, Harry and Bonaro Overstreet refer to gratitude as "the mature emotion." The expression of appreciation is the fruit of considerable cultivation and therefore is seldom found in full bloom among gross people. We are indebted to so many for so much that it behooves us to say "thank you" again and again. No less a man than Paul, the phenomenal Pharisee, unhesitatingly declared: "I am under obligation, both to Greeks and to barbarians, both to the wise and to the foolish; so I am eager to preach the gospel to you also who are in Rome." (Romans 1:14 R.S.V.)

Recall all who have helped us grow in body, mind, and spirit. Endeavor to enumerate friends, known and unknown, who have extended a helping hand. Consider specialists, the wisely skilled persons who keep life at sacred levels. How could we forget those who have loved us into life, nursed our fevers, healed our hurts, and burnished our hopes!

Life is involvement; life is indebtedness. There is no gift equal to the gift of life. There is nothing comparable to wind in your face, sun on your back, the laughter of people, the firm handclasps of friends, the hum of traffic, the satisfaction of work, the challenge of the church, a comfortable home at the day's end, palatable food on the table, clean sheets on the bed, and faith in the future! Life can be increasingly wonderful with the acquisition of the grace of gratitude.

Quite obviously, life is more than a numbered span of years. It is more than prestige, power, or popularity. Certainly it is vastly more than the discoveries of science. Automation is not synonymous with Christian adventure. The acquiring and sharing of generosity and grace keep us close to the heartbeat of God. There is a joy and comfort in knowing we "cannot drift beyond his love and care."

I like Susan Coolidge's encouraging lines:

> Every day is a fresh beginning;
> Listen, my soul, to the glad refrain,
> And, spite of old sorrow and older sinning,
> And puzzles forecasted, and possible pain,
> Take heart with the day and begin again.

How grateful are we for the day's privilege of beginning again? How grateful are we for those who surround us in our tasks? How frequently do we communicate our genuine thanks to those with whom we are associated and in whose debt we stand? A thoughtful letter goes a long way toward communicating appreciation and praise.

In our conceit and complacency we frequently ignore the source of life and our responsibilities as Christians. Ingratitude is a shockingly common sin.

In *As You Like It* Shakespeare has Amiens say:

> Blow, blow, thou winter wind,
> Thou art not so unkind
>   As man's ingratitude;
> Thy tooth is not so keen,
> Because thou art not seen.
>
> . . . .
>
> Freeze, freeze, thou bitter sky,
> That dost not bite so nigh
>   As benefits forgot.

Bread and Butter Letters

One of the first social responsibilities parents endeavor to teach their children is to write "bread and butter" letters. These are simple "thank you" notes for hospitality and entertainment. Though such a letter takes but a few minutes to prepare and post, it speaks volumes. The recipient of any favor or service should promptly register appreciation.

A few years ago we invited the fourth grade from our neighboring elementary school to come to our home for tea. I judge there were about forty children. Though I am reasonably certain the teachers prodded them, we received a "thank you" note from every child, our own included. Some of them were delightful.

DEAR DR. AND MRS. JONES:
Thank you for showing us the Australia movies. They were wonderful pictures. You were nice to invite us over. Thank you again.
Sincerely yours,
R. Z.

DEAR DR. AND MRS. JONES:
I enjoyed every second of it. The slides were very good. Doctor, you took good pictures. I thought your house was beautiful. Your older things were exquisite like the bed and the den with the spinning wheel.
B. I.

Dear Dad:
Thanks for driving us to our house and back to Blackberry Lane. You were nice to show us the slides of Australia. I enjoyed the slides of Australia and the slides of us and our dog. I like the slides of the kangaroos.
Love,
PETER and PAUL

It is earnestly hoped that these children will forever be sensitive to such responsibilities and continue to grow in the grace of gratitude.

OCCASIONS FOR GRATITUDE

The vitality of any program is largely dependent upon the capacity and consecration of the volunteer workers. Those directing the visible life of the church should never cease to communicate messages of praise and gratitude to participants. Deep within, everyone likes to be recognized for his efforts and to be appreciated. A sincere and timely letter builds *esprit de corps* and confidence. Perhaps the following will illustrate possibilities.

To Church School Teachers and Presidents, Elders, and Deacons:

This is simply to say a great big

THANK YOU

Following my letter to you last week about Sunday evening church attendance, the apparent response of everybody last Sunday evening was wonderful! We had one of our best crowds Sunday evening that we've had in a long time, and, to tell the truth, there were so many people from the various class-groups, church school teachers, and church-officers that I could not even make a rough count as to how many were present from each group. This is the kind of attendance we ought to have every Sunday evening, and I hope we can keep it up. I certainly appreciate your response.

The service Sunday evening, unfortunately, ran overtime— in part, because of the special choral group we had and, in part, because of the necessity of introducing the sermon-series. I can assure you that this will not happen again, and that the service will be kept to approximately forty-five minutes.

I hope we will have a similar turnout this Sunday evening and throughout the series on "YOU, YOUR PROBLEMS AND THE BIBLE." Please come yourself—and invite and bring others!

Gratefully yours,[1]

[1] Written by Dr. W. A. Welsh, Minister, East Dallas Christian Church, Dallas. Used by permission.

To Retiring Church Officers

DEAR _____:

This note is to reiterate my appreciation and that of the entire congregation for your leadership as chairman of the Official Board of Union Avenue Christian Church during the year _____. Your tenure was distinctive and dedicated. We are all indebted to you.

With appreciation for our friendship and with all good wishes, I am

Your friend and minister,

For Leadership in Fund-raising

DEAR _____:

This belated and all too brief note is to express the appreciation of the congregation and all of us on the staff, especially myself, for your untiring leadership and effectiveness in our Completion Fund Campaign. We suffered many disappointments, to be sure, but we also had a number of unanticipated victories. We certainly have more money for the program of the church than would have been possible without such an effort.

You gave a tremendous amount of your time, talent and resources to our church and we are grateful.

With appreciation for our friendship and wishing for you and yours the verities of the Christmas season, I am

Gratefully and cordially,

For Accepting New Responsibility

DEAR _____ AND _____:

I am delighted to know that you have agreed to work with the young people of our church. The congregation and the other ministers join me in expressing their gratitude.

The young people of any church, and especially one like ours, are very strategic for they not only determine the caliber of leadership in the future, but the quality of life so essential in the community at large.

Needless to say, youth work can be very discouraging. It is a difficult age, as you well know. However, it has its compensations and I know that you possess the qualities and staying power to help lift the entire level of our youth work. May God bless you as you assume this significant responsibility.

Please be assured of my fullest cooperation.

Gratefully and sincerely,

To One Who Speaks the Timely Word

DEAR _____:

Thank you for your very excellent statement at the Board meeting last night. It helped to create the atmosphere we desired for the meeting, which, of course, was an excellent one.

With all good wishes, I am

Faithfully yours,

To a Staff Member

DEAR _____:

A brief, though sincere word of genuine appreciation for your conduct of the choir last Sunday and for the music in general. It was beautiful! Not that I don't appreciate your services from week to week, but I especially wanted to voice my gratitude to you for last Sunday and ask that you convey it to the choir.

Sincerely,

To Those Not in the Limelight

To _____, _____, _____

MY DEAR FRIENDS:

A brief word of genuine appreciation for your leadership in last night's Thanksgiving dinner. It was a lovely occasion. The food was excellent and well served.

Please convey to your co-workers the gratitude of the church for their services.

Sincerely,

To a Gracious Hostess

MY DEAR FRIENDS:

You were most generous and gracious to open your lovely

home yesterday in the interest of our church. It was a beautiful occasion and was thoroughly enjoyed by all.

I have every reason to believe that these thoughtful teas will greatly encourage friendships in the church and enhance total interest.

With all good wishes, I am

Gratefully and sincerely,

To a Hard and Faithful Worker

DEAR _____:

Before you leave for a well deserved vacation, I write to assure you of our love and gratitude for the many services you render our church. The past year has been a busy one and you have contributed greatly to its effectiveness.

Please forget us while you are away save in your prayers! Have a good vacation.

Sincerely,

To a Church

DEAR DR. JONES:

On behalf of the Hospital, I want to express appreciation to the Union Avenue Christian Church for the gift of flowers which were a part of the Sunday morning services on October 23.

This expression of thoughtfulness is greatly appreciated.

Sincerely yours,[2]

An Appreciation for Congratulations

DEAR CURTIS:

Let me thank you from the bottom of my old academic heart for your word about the Convention Presidency. With help from friends like you I may be able to manage the year in a creditable fashion.

Give me the benefit of your suggestions from time to time.

Sincerely,[3]

[2] Written by Harry M. Piper, Administrator, St. Luke's Hospital, St. Louis. Used by permission.

[3] Written by Dr. Perry E. Gresham, President, Bethany College, Bethany, West Virginia. Used by permission.

Upon Graduation

A young businessman decided to enter the ministry and returned to school at the age of thirty-two. After six years of study and just prior to receiving his B.D. degree, he wrote me this letter:

May 25, 1961

DEAR DR. JONES:

This is to express our appreciation for the help you have given us, both as our minister before you left Vine Street and in helping to ease the financial load of attending college and seminary. We have gained much from your counsel and ministry. It is needless to say that the grant from _____ which you were instrumental in obtaining for us has been of much help in the financial realm.

I plan to graduate from College of the Bible in June, and we will enter full-time service with the Pastoral Unity in Ohio beginning July 1.

Please give our regards to the family.

Sincerely yours,[4]

RECOGNITION AND COMMENDATION

Closely associated with the multitudinous types of thank-you letters is the slightly different letter of special recognition for singular service, accomplishment, or stand in a controversial issue. The minister could and should spend much time writing these letters to members of his congregation, to fellow-Christians throughout the community and around the world.

To a Deserving Showman

While driving in the city one day and listening to the radio I tuned in Arthur Godfrey. I was much impressed by his choice of music and his statement regarding Memorial Day; hence the following letter:

[4] Used by permission.

June 3, 1960

DEAR MR. GODFREY:

For years I have observed your shows with appreciation. I thought the first time you appeared on television after your illness was an excellent demonstration of Christian faith and character.

This letter is to thank you for your splendid sermon given on Memorial Day, though I am sure you did not think you were preaching. To me it was a powerful statement of purpose and an excellent interpretation of permanent values.

Gratefully and sincerely,

To a Businessman of Courage

DEAR MR. ———:

May I commend you for your action on serving persons of all races in your restaurant. I am sure your decision has come after much thought and perhaps conflicting ideas and pressures.

In Grace Church, Jefferson City, Missouri, where I was rector, I went through a similar situation about ten years ago and found that, after the decision was made to do what you have just done, the worst fears of the fearful have never materialized. Fortunately, I have been able to be in parishes which have made this decision through voluntary action of their members, and I rejoice to see persons like you taking what is a risk to some people but which, to others, is our duty.

Respectfully yours,[5]

To a Skilled and Thoughtful Surgeon

DEAR DR. ————:

This note is to reiterate my sincere appreciation for your sympathetic and skilled professional services rendered my wife during hospitalization. You were most considerate and generous in every way and we are thankful.

Should the mysteries of life ever develop to where I or someone in my field could be of assistance to you or anyone in your family, please feel free to command me.

I look forward to making your acquaintance some day.

Gratefully and sincerely,

[5] Written by The Very Reverend Ned Cole, Dean, Christ Church Cathedral, St. Louis. Used by permission.

This physician-surgeon was so extremely thoughtful that I was compelled to write him. For instance, though I had never met him, immediately following the operation, he went to the trouble of locating me by telephone to reassure me.

To State Committeemen

Dear _____:

As we come to the close of another year's work in behalf of the Kingdom of God we pause to thank God for those who make our work an enriching experience of personal satisfaction in witnessing for Christ.

The work that we are seeking to do in behalf of His Kingdom is made possible only because we know that people like you are undergirding our efforts with personal prayer and with personal sacrifice.

We want to express our profound appreciation and sincere gratitude for your personal contribution to His work through the word of our office and staff.

We face the new year with optimism and faith because we know that you will continue to help us meet the great demands and opportunities that God has laid upon our hearts.

Yours in His service,[6]

In this general area of recognitions is correspondence dealing with colleagues and friends as they reach retirement. The older we grow, the more aware we are of the adjustments necessary to face this strategic and frequently discouraging period of life. It requires more than a congenial letter to bridge the gap between regular employment and personal employment. Certainly a letter reassures the individual of our continued concern and love.

To Those Retiring from General Church Work

Dear _____:

_____ informs me that you are about to complete eleven years as chairman of the Florida Conference Board of Education. Certainly your five years of apprenticeship on the Board must have prepared you for such a long period of significant leadership.

[6] Written by James A. Moak, State Secretary, Disciples of Christ, Lexington, Kentucky. Used by permission.

Only a continuous leadership over a number of years can assure genuine educational progress. The effective program in your conference bears testimony to the team relationship between you and _____, the Board itself, and other members of the staff. May the celebration on June 6 be one of many satisfactions. Would that I might be present to express gratitude to you for these years of service to education in Florida Conference.

Cordially yours,[7]

Retiring Editor

MY DEAR FRIEND:

It is my understanding that on February 29, 1956, you will retire as Editor-in-Chief of Church School Literature at the Christian Board of Publication. Your tenure of service in this pivotal position has been significant. You have meant more to the educational consciousness of our brotherhood than you realize. Moreover, you have epitomized your teachings and writings.

You have also been a source of strength and encouragement. Believe it or not, you are partially responsible for my "dabbling" in writing. You published my first article in the *Bethany Church School Guide* and even though it needed your deft touch, you encouraged me to write.

Knowing you as I do, March will not bring retirement, but simply a rearrangement of activities and responsibilities.

I wish you and _____ a most pleasant and safe world trip. You boys be careful in gay Paree!

With appreciation for our friendship, I am

Most cordially,

ENCOURAGEMENT

Evidently Paul, the great Christian correspondent and missionary, was considerably impressed by Barnabas, a prominent Hellenistic-Jewish Christian. We are reminded that this man was originally named Joseph, but his colleagues appropriately assigned to him the surname Barnabas. Interestingly enough, scholars tell us that an accurate translation of the word "Barnabas" means *son of encourage-*

[7] Written by Leon M. Adkins, General Secretary, Methodist Church Board of Education, Nashville. Used by permission.

ment. Apparently Barnabas lived up to his name. This is a continuing need and a compelling vocation. Virtually everyone of our acquaintance has some problem, some gnawing concern with which he must live day and night. A word of encouragement at the right time may well be the difference between despair and dedication.

It came to me that one of the twelve-year-old boys in the church had failed to make the little-league baseball team and that he was heartbroken, whereupon I wrote him a letter.

To a Twelve-Year-Old Boy

DEAR _____:

A little bird told me—and what bird would be better qualified at the moment than a Cardinal—of your discouragement in not being immediately assigned to a position on your baseball team. This may be your first real bump with discouragement; thus this word of encouragement.

As we grow older we learn many things and one is that failure is usually the first step toward success. Someone has said that success is failure turned inside out. How well I remember my disappointment at not making our little baseball team and how proud I was when I made the high school team.

I shall never forget when Curtis failed to make the high school baseball squad as a freshman, yet because of his perseverance, within two weeks the coach recalled him and in his junior year he pitched a one hitter.

All of this is to say that we all have our ups and downs and coaches and managers make mistakes in their decisions. I wonder how the manager of the Phillies feels after trading off Don Caldwell!

I would suggest that you keep working at your baseball and preferably with someone older and better than yourself so that you will be constantly challenged to perform at your best. With your size and spirit, you are bound to succeed.

I thought you might be interested in the following success story:

Nothing so closely resembles pride as discouragement. When a truly great person fails at an objective, he does not give way to discouragement. He tries again. One man whose greatness shone in persistent trying again in the face of failure left this record:

Failed in business, 1831
Defeated for legislature, 1832
Again failed in business, 1833
Elected to legislature, 1834
Defeated for speaker, 1838
Defeated for elector, 1840
Defeated for Congress, 1843
Elected to Congress, 1846
Defeated for Congress, 1848
Defeated for vice president, 1856
Defeated for Senate, 1858

Here, indeed, is a record which might cause any man to lose faith in himself and hope for his ideals. Fortunately the man who compiled it lost neither faith nor hope. He tried again—and we honor his memory. He was Abraham Lincoln, elected—in 1860—to serve as President of the United States.

Sincerely,

Sudden Illness

A fine couple had been shocked at the news that their minister-son was facing serious surgery seven hundred miles away. I was moved to write this letter with the hope that they would have it upon their arrival.

My dear Friends:

A brief word to express the hope that you had a safe trip and that you are encouraged by your son's condition. Please be assured of the thoughts and prayers of the members and ministers of your church.

May God abundantly bless and sustain you and yours.

Sincerely,

To the Mother of a Handicapped Child

We are all familiar with parents who must live with handicapped children. Some rise to glorious heights of tenderness and love, while others become embittered and resentful, and turn from the church.

Words, words, words. They are my stock in trade, so to speak, and I am sometimes chary of them. So I ask you again: what can I say to you and to every young mother whose cross has taken to itself the shape and substance of a small child who is retarded, physically and mentally and spiritually, one of the bitterest blows of all for married-love to receive. I can, at least, send to you and to her a little letter that appeared in *The Machinist* dated November 22, 1956, which a railway-man loaned to me. Even a minister of religion, as I am, can find beauty in unexpected places as well as *saints in Caesar's household*. It was written to Dr. William A. Sawyer, an IAM consultant, who conducts a regular human relations and health problem column, in the weekly paper named. Here it is *in toto*:

DEAR DR. _____:

In the July 5, 1956 issue of *The Machinist* you wrote about the mentally retarded child. My husband and I have been the parents of a retarded boy for five years. I feel that life really began when he came. I felt God must have had a lot of faith in us as parents to trust something so fragile to our care.

Somehow it seems more important to serve God, than to look upon our child as a tragedy. God's promise to man is to give us our needs, not our wants. With our child we felt that something very beautiful had come. Our lives seem so rich and full we enjoy our problems. Our child's progress is like that of a normal child only much slower.

With the help of our school psychologist, a parent group has been started in our town. We hope to hold a class every Saturday this September for the mentally retarded children. In the future I hope swimming classes will be started for these children. There is a lot of research to be done.

Every parent of a retarded child is greatly needed. I feel it is God's way of telling us, man's work is not yet done. If this letter will help anyone, please use it. I hope it will give someone a lift.

Sincerely yours,
A MOTHER [8]

[8] Dr. Johnstone G. Patrick, Minister, First Presbyterian Church, Sayre, Pennsylvania, and International Association of Machinists, publishers of *The Machinist*. Used by permission.

This is a tremendously helpful letter which emanates from the heart of one who knows whereof she speaks.

To Your Minister

Did it ever occur to you that, generally speaking, the minister is the only person in the congregation who does not have a minister? He, too, becomes discouraged. He, too, has problems. He, too, needs encouragement. During a very difficult time in my ministry I received this heartening letter from a dear member of our congregation.

DEAR DR. JONES:

If the problems seem a little big, just remember a little guy can solve little problems. We knew our problems were big—that's why we needed a big man to help solve them.

As you get a chance to "dig around" you'll find there are a lot of us ready to help you.

Sincerely,[9]

[9] Used by permission.

7

Congratulations, Comfort, Condolence

In his *The Walk with Destiny*, Sir Winston L. Spencer Churchill says, "I have been a journalist half my lifetime and I have earned my living by selling words, and I hope thoughts."

The ancient writer of Proverbs knew the power and beauty of language when he said, "A word fitly spoken is like apples of gold in a setting of silver" (Proverbs 25:11).

A good letter should be well worded, for words are ambassadors. Equally important, it should convey a central thought. This is particularly true in times of exceptional joy or devastating sorrow. A well-conceived letter can be an encouraging, comforting, and permanent form of communication which the reader will review again and again.

CONGRATULATIONS

Churches could profit by imitating those institutions and businesses that have a staff person responsible for sifting the news and communicating pertinent information and greetings to their clients, associates and friends. This is more than a public-relations gimmick. It could well be the beginning of a more significant relationship. Virtually every accomplishment and occasion for rejoicing merits a congratulatory letter. It may be typed or handwritten. The only prerequisites are that it glow with sincerity and warmth.

A New Church

MY DEAR FRIEND:
Congratulations and best wishes for the forthcoming dedicatory services. The ministers and members of Union Avenue join me in expressing to you and your people our great delight at this significant accomplishment and pray that you will have a wonderful day and an ever increasing ministry to our Lord.

Sincerely,

Dedication of Facilities

DEAR CURTIS:
On behalf of the churches of the Disciples of Christ, let me extend to you our heartiest congratulations on the achievement which the Union Avenue Christian Church is celebrating during the month of March.

I will be denied the privilege of sharing in this meaningful experience with you and your people, but be assured of our prayers and best wishes.

Cordially,[1]

To a High School Senior

DEAR _____:
Congratulations on being accepted at MIT! If you could not settle on Yale, then MIT would be pretty close to the right decision. I know that you will enjoy it and I shall follow your academic growth with pride and pleasure.

With all good wishes, I am
Expectantly and sincerely,

Convention President

DEAR _____:
Being in the balcony last night, together with the tremendous press of people between "me and thee" prevented my coming to

[1] Written by Dr. Granville T. Walker, Minister, University Christian Church, Fort Worth. Used by permission.

the platform to congratulate you on a splendid convention.
I hope you and _____ will have a restful stay in _____.
With all good wishes to your family and with appreciation for
our friendship, I am

Most cordially,

Church Election

DEAR BISHOP _____:

This note is to extend to you congratulations and best wishes
of the ministers and members of Union Avenue Christian Church
on being elected Presiding Bishop of the Protestant Episcopal
Church.

We are very proud of you. Please be assured of our love and
prayers.

Sincerely,

DEAR _____:

Congratulations on being elected president of our International
Convention!

You will make us a splendid leader. Please be assured of our
fullest cooperation.

With all good wishes, I am

Cordially,

Recipient of Honorary Degree

MY DEAR JUDGE _____:

Congratulations on receiving the Doctor of Laws Degree from
Culver-Stockton College!

We were invited to attend, but a crowded schedule prevented
the pleasure.

With all good wishes to you and yours, I am

Very respectfully yours,

Mother's Day

DEAR MRS. _____:

Congratulations on being honored as Mother-of-the-Year at
Central Woodward!

We often think of our ministry in Detroit and can never divorce it from your faithful support and work. May God bless you on this high day and the church we love so much.

Sybil and the boys join me in affectionate good wishes.

Sincerely,

New Minister in Community

DEAR DR. _____:

Congratulations on being called to lead the great Third Baptist Church in St. Louis, and welcome to our city!

We have been in St. Louis about four years and are beginning to feel at home. If there is anything I can do at all to assist you, please command me.

I look forward to making your acquaintance and that of your family. May God richly bless and guide you in your significant work.

Sincerely,

Business and Professional Promotions

DEAR _____:

Congratulations on being called to the presidency of the Disciples Historical Society! I think it is a happy choice. Knowing your father's great interest in history, I have a feeling that he, too, is happy over your decision and that of the Society.

Needless to say, I hope you may find your place in Vine Street Christian Church.

With all good wishes to you and your good wife, I am

Most cordially,

Baseball Manager

DEAR ALVIN:

Congratulations on being chosen manager of the San Francisco Giants! This is a tremendous honor and recognition of your capacities, and we are happy for you. If one is to believe what he reads about the Giants these days, it required considerable courage on your part; knowing you as I do, I have no doubt that you will lead them competently and victoriously. It is a source of real satisfaction to know that a man of your character will be the Field General of the Giants.

Do you need a Chaplain? My guess is that you are going to
need some prayers beyond those that will be offered proudly by
the Southern Baptists!

You will be interested to know that our David is in Hiram College, a sophomore and playing football, while his twin DeWitt is
playing at Yale. Curtis is a first year man at Yale Divinity School.
I visited with Curtis and DeWitt last week. They, too, were delighted that the Giants named you manager, and send greetings.

Very cordially,

Personal Accomplishment

A New Author

DEAR _____:

Congratulations on your new book *The Christian Layman and
His Church!* I have been through it. It looks very good and it reads
well. You were kind to send me an autographed copy. I appreciate
it.

With all good wishes, I am

Cordially,

College Student

DEAR _____:

Congratulations on being elected to *Who's Who in the American Colleges and Universities!* Members and ministers of your
church are very proud of you and your record and wish for you
every blessing as you pursue graduate studies.

With pastoral good wishes, I am

Sincerely,

Graduation

DEAR _____:

My hearty congratulations upon your graduation! This is a
significant occasion in your life, and all of us in _____ are
justly proud of you.

Of course, the Church will have its influence upon your future.
The reality of the meaning of Jesus' life has become very evident
to you. By all means, you will want to keep it uppermost in your
life.

I hope that you will always count me as your friend, as well

as your minister. I am very much interested in your future and covet any opportunity to help you. May God bless you always!
Faithfully yours,[2]

Wedding Anniversary

MY DEAR FRIENDS:

Congratulations on your twenty-fifth wedding anniversary! It has been a pleasure to have known you across the years, to observe your maturing love and the growth of your splendid family. You hold an honored place in our church and in our hearts.
With pastoral good wishes, I am
Very sincerely yours,

Anniversary of Death

DEAR _____:

It has been a year since your wonderful partner was called home. I know the past few months have been very difficult for you and the family, yet you have borne your sorrow with grace and dignity. May God richly bless you as you strive to serve as mother and father to your children.
Please be assured of the love and the availability of the members and the ministers of your church.
Prayerfully and sincerely,

Golden Anniversary of a Business

DEAR _____:

Congratulations on the Fiftieth Anniversary of the Christian Board of Publication! You and your colleagues are to be commended for phenomenal progress and splendid service. May God continue to bless and strengthen you as you labor among us.
With great appreciation for your leadership and for our friendship, I am
Cordially,

[2] Written by Dr. Myron C. Cole, Hollywood-Beverly Christian Church, Hollywood, California. Used by permission.

Birth

DEAR MR. AND MRS. _____:
Congratulations on the arrival of _____ [name of child].
We pray that he will develop in wisdom and stature and in favor
with God and man.
With pastoral good wishes, I am
Sincerely,

COMFORT

There is a vast variety of illnesses, and at one time or another
everyone becomes ill. Church people are not immune. The sympathetic pastor will be alert to sickness among those of his congregation and will communicate accordingly. However appropriate the
note or letter, it is not a substitute for a personal visit; yet there are
cases where not even the minister is permitted to call, and his sole
means of conveying concern is through correspondence.

Chronic Illness

DEAR MRS. _____:
Thank you for your letter. I am sorry to hear of your mother's
continued illness. Please be assured of our prayers and good
wishes. If there is any service the church can render, please command us.
With all good wishes, I am
Prayerfully yours,

Hospitalization During Long Illness

DEAR MRS. _____:
You were very thoughtful to call me today to advise me of
your mother's condition. Please be assured that your church and
ministers will be thinking of you and her during these trying days.
If there is anything any of us can do, please feel free to call.
Praying God's richest blessings upon you and yours, I am
Sincerely,

Accident

Dear Mrs. _____:

How very sorry we are to hear of your accident. I do hope you are more comfortable and that you are making steady and rapid progress. I shall be by to see you in a few days. Meanwhile, be assured of our prayers and best wishes.

Sincerely,

Invalid

Dear _____:

To be confined to one's bed for a quarter of a century is a long time. As I have tried to say to you so many times, you are a peculiar physician, in that your alertness to the needs of others, your ability to keep in touch with your church and business by telephone, your voluminous correspondence, your graciousness in receiving callers, your ability to divert conversation from yourself to the outside world is indeed an inspiration. And yet, I suspect there are times when you wonder about your illness and why you must see the world only from your window and from television.

The problem of suffering is age-old. There were those who believed it was associated with sin and that God used this painful method of punishing His children. Intelligent Christianity does not attribute illness to the wrath of God, but places it where it belongs, human frailty and misfortune. No one who has been privileged to know you would doubt for a moment your integrity, good will and Christian faith.

The deeper question, I think, is not why we suffer, but what philosophy of life we reflect. Some people, apparently, do not have the resources to cope with crippling circumstances and thus use them as a façade rather than a means of demonstrating genuineness. The stewardship of suffering is a distinctive mark of a great person. Did not our Lord Jesus Christ suffer beyond all comprehension? Yet through suffering love he revealed the glory and goodness of God.

In my judgment you are the ablest minister in our community. Please be assured of my prayers and availability at any time.

Faithfully yours,

Message in the Margin

People live with all kinds of problems, some of them far more sorrowful than death. To be able to write a comforting word is a significant ministry. A personal memorandum in the right place can be more powerful than the longest letter.

In *Prescription for Anxiety*, Leslie D. Weatherhead shares an experience he had with the noted journalist, Hugh Redwood. It seems that Mr. Redwood was facing very trying circumstances that demanded a difficult decision. He hardly knew where to turn. While visiting in the home of a friend, prior to a speaking engagement, his thoughtful host suggested that he go upstairs for a while and rest before his lecture. The weary and troubled man gladly accepted the opportunity to withdraw from people. His perceptive friend had prepared the room for his coming. A cheery fire was blazing on the hearth, a comfortable chair was appropriately placed and on the table near his chair was a Bible opened at the 59th Psalm. "My God in His steadfast love will meet me. . . ." Then by this tenth verse was written in pencil this comforting interpretation, "My God in His loving kindness shall meet me at every corner." It was a most helpful discovery. Mr. Redwood made the right decision. He turned his corner successfully.

At one time or another everyone has to turn dangerous and costly corners. It may be a family problem, a reversal in business, or a sudden and prolonged illness. While death demands comfort, it is by no means the only time in life when one needs to be reassured and comforted.

Storm Tragedy

DEAR MR. _____:

How very sorry we were to hear of the consequences of the terrifying storm and the lives it claimed. Please be assured of our affectionate thoughts and prayers.

I know that you will accept this blow with characteristic strength and grace. May God enable you and your family to continue the pilgrimage in trust and Christian faith.

Understandingly yours,

Bereavement

DEAR MR. _____:

This note is to convey the affection and prayers of your church and ministers during these days of heartache. May God abundantly bless you and yours.

With pastoral good wishes, I am

Sincerely,

Here are two helpful paragraphs dealing with an individual who resented his situation.

It is human and natural to feel resentment when we seem to be the victims of unjust behavior on the part of others. But it is comforting to know that we can unburden it all to God, knowing that He can soften our hearts and give us His peace, even to the extent that we try to understand those who have hurt us. . . .

When resentment enters our hearts, justified or not, it seems to create guilt feelings and guilt feelings tend to estrange us from God and also cause us to feel that "the whole world is against us." Therefore, we need God's help in order to forgive and once more feel in tune with Him and with life.[3]

DEAR _____:

Please be assured that your church and ministers are thinking of you and your family during these trying days. Love always carries a heavy load. Your days have been crowded with concern and anxiety.

Prayerfully and cordially,

CONDOLENCE

Man fears death. He has always been more confident of physical protection than spiritual security. To walk amid the pyramids of Egypt is to realize that they are gigantic and costly tombs elaborately equipped for residence in the next world. Only a haunting fear of

---

[3] Written by Dr. Norman Vincent Peale, Minister, Marble Collegiate Church, New York. Used by permission.

death would drive a king to spend his lifetime preparing for survival. Death has been memorialized, commercialized, and sentimentalized throughout history.

Though the Christian believes in a future life that defies description yet satisfies his longings, though the Christian believes that Jesus arose from the dead and that "he is the resurrection and the life," nevertheless he suffers and frequently agonizes under the visitation of death.

When Jesus and his disciples came to the city of Nain, they encountered a funeral party. A widow had lost her only son. When the Lord noticed the distraught woman, he was filled with compassion and charged her not to weep. "And he came and touched the bier, and the bearers stood still. And he said, 'Young man, I say to you, arise.' And the dead man sat up, and began to speak. And he gave him to his mother." (Luke 7:14–15)

This is a comforting and mighty miracle. Jesus met death in the narrow gate at Nain. Death and life always meet in a narrow place, and Jesus is there to comfort and sustain. To be able to believe this and to communicate this faith is the heart of condolence.

Though death is common, there is something distinctive about each homegoing that requires personal understanding and attention.

Soldier Overseas

Dear _____:

By the time you receive this letter you will have had the saddening message of the passing of your dear Mother. I want you to know that everything scientifically and spiritually possible was done for her, and that we all mourn her death. We were touched by your absence, knowing the extremely close relationship which you and your mother enjoyed.

This, I know, will be your major battle of the war, and I pray God that you may have the courage, strength and faith to fight it through to a victorious understanding and acceptance.

Assuring you of my deep personal sympathy and of the affection and prayers of the church, I am

Sincerely,

Dear Mr. _____:

Because I was not able to reach you by telephone this morning, this note is an attempt to convey the sympathy and prayers of your church and staff in the homegoing of your mother.

It is a most difficult and revealing experience and only those of us who have gone through it can fully comprehend such a loss.

Prayerfully and sincerely,

To Parents

DEAR _____ AND _____:

I was distressed to read in _____ of the death of your beloved daughter, Peggy.

None of us, your friends, can walk with you along the deep path of grief which the death of such a lovely girl brings to you. Grief in its depths is always extremely personal. But we can share with you a genuine sympathy, human understanding and love, and it is these which I wish to express to you both.

I want you to know that I shall remember you most earnestly in prayer, that the Lord will bring comfort and peace to your wounded hearts.

It is my personal faith, that while you feel that you have lost Peggy, in the deepest sense of the word you have not. She will always be near and dear to you, and finally when your own lives are completed on earth you will be reunited with her, never to be separated again.

My wife, Ruth, joins me in sincere friendship to you both.

Cordially yours,[4]

The following letter was sent to a young lady who grew up in our church and whose marriage took her to a distant state. Her father, president of the Official Board of our congregation, died suddenly. A winter blizzard prevented her attendance at the funeral.

DEAR _____:

We were all severely shocked and saddened by your father's sudden passing. Moreover, we regret that you and _____ cannot attend the service tomorrow, though we fully appreciate the situation and will be thinking of you.

. . . .

Your father was a remarkably fine man, a great Christian and churchman, and his ministry among us will be long remembered.

[4] Written by Dr. Norman Vincent Peale, Minister, Marble Collegiate Church, New York. Used by permission.

Your mother is doing wonderfully well, as are the other members of your family.

Love and best wishes,

Another very difficult type of letter to write is to the widow of a minister friend.

Minister's Widow

DEAR MRS. _____:

It was with sincere regret and shock that I heard of _____'s death today. I was very fond of him. In my judgment, he was one of the truly great ministers of our brotherhood. May the God whom he served so faithfully, bless you and sustain you.

Sybil joins me in prayerful good wishes to you and your family.

Sincerely,

Neither the minister nor his family is spared bereavement. Frequently they too must walk down the valley of the shadows, and they too need the ministry of condolence. Here are two letters from friends of mine in the ministry, written at the time of my mother's death.

From Fellow Ministers

DEAR CURTIS:

I was away when your message came bringing the sad news of your mother's passing. It was, therefore, impossible for me to get down for the funeral which I deeply regret.

You and your family have my sincere sympathy. I can appreciate your keen sense of loss. Though I had neglected to write until now, I had thought of you many times this past week.

We are bound together in Christian faith in special tenderness in times like this. Please share my thoughts with all your family.

Sincerely,[5]

[5] Written by Dr. R. B. Montgomery, President, College of the Bible, Lexington, Kentucky. Used by permission.

MY DEAR CURTIS:

So your dear mother has gone home. There is something unspeakably sad about that, and yet something thrillingly triumphant. When a cable came to me from Adelaide, South Australia, some ten years ago, informing me that my own mother had passed away, it left a great empty space against the sky, and a painful sense of vacancy in my heart. And yet, as I reflected calmly about it, I could see the beauty of it, the promise of it, the assurance it brings that life goes on forever beyond the frontiers of earth and time.

My mother's lovely life is to me proof enough that she is living still in happiness and triumph. I cannot conceive that a universe with any goodness and justice at its heart would let her down. If it did, I would feel like using the defiant language of Stanley Jones: "If, at the end, I should find that there is no future life, I would look the universe straight in the face and say: 'I thought better of you. I thought you made sense. Now I see you make nonsense. I'm sorry. You've let me down. In this hour of dissolution I'm better than you are. I thought morality had eternal significance. It doesn't. But I thought thoughts higher than you sustain, so I am superior to you. You are insignificant—not I.'"

There's a spiritual cosmos, as well as a physical one; and if the physical cosmos is at such infinite pains to conserve its physical energy or energies, how much more should the spiritual cosmos concern itself with the eternal preservation of those priceless spiritual values which flourished in such loveliness and radiance in the souls of your dear mother and mine.

Our deep and affectionate sympathy to you and your dear ones in this bereavement, and may our Good Father keep you always in His loving care.

Faithfully and fraternally yours,[6]

[6] Written by the late Dr. C. M. Gordon, Norfolk. Used by permission.

8

Invitations, Acceptances, Regrets, Resignations

INVITATIONS

A letter of invitation is a skillful combination of spirit and style. It should be warm and friendly. Psychologically, a letter of invitation should be pleasing, thus motivating an affirmative response. It should flatter sufficiently to gain attention, and yet it should be sincere and direct.

Here are some representative examples:

Rev. G. Curtis Jones
7931 Gannon Avenue
St. Louis 30, Missouri

DEAR MR. JONES:

We discovered your name in the summer issue of *Stewardship Associates Bulletin*. My purpose in writing you at this time is twofold.

First, the subject of your new book is intriguing. We, in Illinois Council of Churches' circles, are keenly interested in the whole stewardship field, and a copy of your new book will be secured as soon as it is available.

The second purpose of this letter is to inquire if you might be

118

available for a program assignment in the forthcoming Stewardship Institute December 1, 2, 1960. The enclosed tentative program outline will give you an idea of the nature and purpose of
this Institute. The specific assignment would be—address: "A
Pastor Looks at Stewardship" which is scheduled for Friday, December 2 at 9:30 A.M. (See enclosed marked Program.)

I shall look forward to hearing from you very soon.

Cordially yours,[1]

The sender ventured to write because he found me in print.
Thus he wrote with restraint. Though formal, this letter is comprehensive and clear.

DEAR _____:

At a meeting of our Evangelism Committee some weeks ago,
I suggested that we extend to you an invitation to conduct for us
evangelistic services around the Easter season of 1961. This recommendation from the Evangelism Committee was unanimously
accepted by the Administrative Board last evening. I feel that your
services in leading this church in a week of preaching would be
most beneficial. Also, I felt that it would be necessary to get our
name on your calendar a good time ahead of schedule.

If you can see fit to be with us for one week to ten days, I
would most deeply appreciate it.

With kindest regards, I remain

Sincerely yours,[2]

This exploratory letter of invitation is from a fellow minister.
Quite obviously he wanted me to visit his church, inasmuch as he
wrote two years in advance, allowing ample freedom in choice of
dates. This is a cordial way to secure a speaker.

DEAR CURTIS:

On behalf of the Divinity School faculty, which customarily
has chosen the Baccalaureate preacher for Commencement exercises at Vanderbilt, I am writing to invite you to be the speaker
on Sunday, June 4, 1961, at 11:00 A.M. Here at Vanderbilt we do

[1] Written by Vernon H. MacNeill, Executive Secretary, Illinois Council of
Churches, Springfield. Used by permission.

[2] Written by B. Frank Leggett, Jr., Minister, First Christian Church, Rocky
Mount, North Carolina. Used by permission.

not have both a Baccalaureate sermon and a Commencement address, but rather one sermon in the context of a service of worship to which all the graduates and their families are invited. This service will be held in our largest auditorium.

I fully realize how busy you must be with all of your duties but it has been my desire for some time that you fulfill this very important engagement in the life of our university. We have enjoyed addresses of superb quality and know that you, if you accept this invitation, will continue the good tradition. I should point out that the graduates include not only those receiving the A.B. degree, but also those receiving degrees in medicine, law, engineering, nursing, humanities, and Divinity.

Naturally the university will pay for all of your expenses involved in travel and accommodations, and also offer you an honorarium of _____. We hope very much that you are not already engaged for that day and that you will feel disposed to accept this invitation.

With kindest personal regards and sincere best wishes, I remain

Respectfully yours,[3]

Though Dr. Norton's friendship inevitably shines through in this letter, it is nevertheless an excellently worded invitation. It is clear, flattering, and demanding.

DEAR _____:

The General Commission on Chaplains and Armed Forces Personnel will conduct Protestant Chaplain Retreats during the calendar year of 1962. Protestant chaplains on an active duty status with the United States Army, the United States Navy, the United States Air Force and the Veterans Administration are eligible to participate in these retreats.

Your denominational headquarters has especially recommended and urged that we invite you to represent your denomination in this Protestant Chaplain Retreat Program. We would like to have you participate in the retreat to be held at Spring Mill Inn, Mitchell, Indiana, on 19–22 February 1962.

Enclosed is the initial work paper presenting a complete outline for the retreats. As you read the program, it can be noted that we hope to achieve our purpose for the retreats through (1)

[3] Written by Dr. Herman Norton, Acting Dean, The Divinity School, Vanderbilt University, Nashville. Used by permission.

worship, (2) instruction and (3) by the conduct of a forum discussion group dealing with practical and realistic problems encountered by the chaplain in his relationship with people. I earnestly believe that the most valuable aspect of any Chaplain Retreat will be measured by the workable and matter-of-fact guidance the participant receives. The chaplain needs help and advice which will aid him in meeting the daily problems of his ministry. You will note that I have marked the items on the outline which pertain to the forum discussions.

The General Commission provides an honorarium and will pay all travel costs to and from the retreat. I do hope that you can realize how greatly the Protestant chaplains will appreciate the opportunity and privilege of having you as a Retreat Leader. Following our receipt of your acceptance, I shall provide you with more detailed information.

Sincerely yours,[4]

To add warmth to the invitation, the Chaplain wrote a gracious P.S. in longhand.

Within the Congregation

It is evident that there is a different approach in writing letters of invitation to members of one's own congregation. Here are a few:

DEAR FIRST BAPTIST FRIEND:

"The harvest is past, the summer is ended, and we are not saved" (Jeremiah 8:20) is one of the most poignant verses in the entire Bible. Thank God it is one that we can do something about this fall in the life of our church. *The Church Officers Retreat* Saturday, September 8th, 10:00 to 4:00 P.M. will enable us to lay plans to see that many are saved this fall and many brought into a closer walk with our Lord Jesus Christ.

Our Standing Committee, Board of Trustees, and Board of Deacons have enthusiastically endorsed the program for this retreat. When I presented the challenge of this program to Mr. Alvan T. Fuller, he was most happy to invite all of the church officers and the four officers of each organization with their hus-

---

[4] Written by Chaplain Glenn J. Witherspoon, Director, Department of Chaplaincy Services, The General Commission on Chaplains and Armed Forces Personnel, Washington. Used by permission.

bands, wives, or escorts to be his guests for this retreat at the Hotel Farragut, Rye Beach, New Hampshire. The hotel is about one-half mile north of Mr. Fuller's home. You take Route 1 to the New highway. At the New Hampshire interchange for Hampton Beach, take Route 101-C to the ocean, turn left and it is about two miles. The hotel is providing adequate meeting and assembly rooms. In case of rainy weather, the clam bake will be in the dining hall.

As I mentioned in my letter of June 9th it will be an old-fashioned clam bake with lobster, roast corn, watermelon and all the fixings. We are very fortunate in securing outstanding leadership, Dr. Carl Herrick and Edwin Tuller.

Apart from last minute changes the schedule is enclosed. Be sure and bring it with you. You can understand why it is quite essential for you to *fill out the enclosed postal* and *return it to us as soon as possible* so that the hotel might know how many to expect. We are quite anxious to have as near 100% of our church leaders as possible. If you have any question about who is invited, bring them! We want especially husbands, wives, and escorts of our church officers to make the day an outing as well as a period of Christian development.

Mr. Arnold Hawkins will be available for further information if you need it. Telephone him at the church, MA 4-2745, or his home, MA 2-8986. He will have charge of transportation. If you need transportation, get in touch with Mr. Hawkins.

God will bless us through our church in proportion to our faith. I am sure that the early planning and spiritual renewal that the retreat will bring will be most helpful in preparing us for our fall activities.

Cordially your pastor,[5]

DEAR _____:

We are happy indeed to have you in the fellowship of Union Avenue Christian Church and trust that by now you are beginning to feel at home.

We like to recognize and orient our new members as faithfully as possible, and I write to invite you to be our dinner-guest Sunday evening, at six o'clock. The informal meal will be served in the dining room. A profitable program will follow.

The enclosed card is for your convenience to notify us of your intention to attend the new members dinner. We hope you will

[5] Written by Dr. Hillyer H. Straton, Minister, First Baptist Church, Malden, Massachusetts. Used by permission.

make a special effort to be present. Whether you can attend or not, please return the card promptly. Will you let us hear from you by Tuesday?

Thanking you for your cooperation and looking forward to seeing you at this special occasion, and with pastoral good wishes, I am

Sincerely,

DEAR STUDENT FRIEND:

The Joneses would like to invite you and our other college students to an evening at the Manse, 7931 Gannon Avenue, University City, Sunday, from seven-thirty to nine-thirty.

You are free, of course, to bring a friend or an escort. We anticipate an enjoyable time together.

The enclosed card is to confirm your attendance. Please reply by _____ [date].

Happy Holidays!

Sincerely,

DEAR MEMBERS AND FRIENDS OF BETHANY:

This letter is being sent to every family of Bethany Church with the hope that every member will do his utmost to attend the Wednesday evening Lenten services. Lent has been called the "evangelistic season" of the Evangelical and Reformed Church and we will need your help in making these services significant and worth-while.

Enclosed you will find two Lenten folders giving sermon topics. Your pastors will endeavor to make these sermons interesting and helpful. On page two of the folder you will find some of the suggestions which will make the Lenten season significant for all of our families.

Since we are conducting a membership campaign in the church and all of its organizations beginning with Ash Wednesday, we are asking that you do your utmost to win someone to Christ and His Church during the Lenten season. An application blank is appended to the enclosed folder which you may use. Additional folders will be found in the church narthex.

Please have every member of your family read this letter or, better still, read it together at the dinner table.

Very sincerely yours,[6]

_____

[6] Written by Dr. Walter A. Scheer, Pastor, Bethany Evangelical and Reformed Church (United Church of Christ), St. Louis. Used by permission.

DEAR FRIEND:

Under the auspices of the Men's Club of Temple Israel, the Twenty-Fourth Institute of Judaism for Christian Clergy will be held on Monday, April 24, at Temple Israel, Kingshighway and Washington Avenues.

The Institute Speaker this year will be Professor Lou H. Silberman, Professor of Jewish Literature and Thought at Vanderbilt University, Nashville, Tennessee. His subjects will be: "Rabbinic Insights into some Gospel Passages," and "Jewish Backgrounds of the Last Supper."

Please let me know on the enclosed postal card that I may use your name on the program of the Institute as an Honorary Sponsor. As soon as the program is printed, you will receive an invitation to attend this Institute, and I look forward to seeing you then.

With many appreciations for your cooperation, and cordial greetings, I remain,

Sincerely yours,[7]

General State secretaries and church executives write a great number of letters reminding their colleagues of important meetings and conferences.

DEAR FRIEND:

The annual State-Wide Program Planning Conference is being held at the Baptist Eagle Eyrie, Lynchburg, _____ [dates]. At this meeting, we hope to have all of the Agencies working within Virginia, planning together the program of activities for the Churches in Virginia for the year 1961–62.

As a member of one of the several groups being brought together to this work, I wish to extend to you a personal invitation to be present, and to assist your group and the total work of the Church in Virginia, in making possible a united program and approach to the churches.

The Virginia Christian Missionary Society is underwriting the entire program of this Planning Conference. In order that we may conserve our resources, we are asking that you travel in car pools, and there is enclosed with this letter a list of the people who are invited to attend. We will pay the expenses of those sharing in a car pool. . . .

[7] Written by Dr. Ferdinand M. Isserman, Rabbi, Temple Israel, St. Louis. Used by permission.

You will be receiving additional word concerning the Planning Conference from those executives under whom you will work. We trust you will heed these communications and at the same time indicate to us your presence or not. There is enclosed a card on which you will indicate your presence at the meeting and the name of the Board you represent.

It will be necessary that we have your reply no later than _____ [date], in order to make our room assignments and to know how many to expect for meals.

We trust that you will join with us in this Program Planning for the Churches of Virginia.

Sincerely yours,[8]

ACCEPTANCE

To Participate in a Planning Retreat

As a general rule, letters of acceptance are brief. For example:

DEAR DON:

I will be most happy to attend your planning retreat at _____ on _____ [date].

I understand that I will lead a discussion with the deacons in an understanding of their responsibilities. Please send the tentative schedule for this retreat when it is prepared.

Respectfully yours,[9]

Acceptance of Speaking Engagement

DEAR DR. JONES:

It was indeed a great pleasure to receive your kind invitation to speak at a dinner meeting at your church on Wednesday evening, February 18. I will be glad to accept this invitation and I appreciate your allowing me the freedom to choose my topic. Because of my particular interest in the field of mental health I imagine that what I have to say will relate to that area.

[8] Written by H. Myron Kauffman, Executive Secretary, The Virginia Christian Missionary Society, Christian Churches of Virginia, Richmond. Used by permission.

[9] Written by Lester D. Palmer, Christian Church of Kentucky, Lexington. Used by permission.

I have sent the only available glossy prints of myself (two) to Dr. Wagner of the Church Federation with the request that he send you one of them when he is finished with it. I regret that I do not have any other prints on hand. Enclosed please find the biographical sketch which you requested.

Until February then, may I extend to you my very best wishes.

Sincerely yours,[10]

Acceptance of Resignation

DEAR MRS. _____:

Before leaving the city I wish to acknowledge and accept your letter of resignation as church _____ [officer] and to reiterate my appreciation and that of the staff and congregation for your valuable ministry to Union Avenue Christian Church. You have been most cooperative and loyal.

With every good wish to you and yours, I am

Sincerely,

Conditional Acceptance

DEAR MR. _____:

Thank you for your letter of December 31 and for the invitation to be the guest speaker at your State Convention, March 9-11.

I shall be very glad to be of service to you, provided you can arrange my speeches for Thursday and Friday, as I have to be back in St. Louis on Saturday. Therefore, I would need to leave Boise either late Friday night or early Saturday morning. It would be necessary for me to fly.

I should appreciate clarification on the number and time of the addresses I am to deliver.

With all good wishes, I am

Cordially,

There are occasions when one must accept an invitation conditionally. While at first blush it may appear to be dictatorial and arbitrary, it should not be so considered.

[10] Written by Dr. Kenneth W. Mann, Associate Chaplain, The Hospital of the Good Samaritan, Los Angeles. Used by permission.

REGRET

Few busy men can accept all the invitations that come to them. Therefore letters of declination are frequently required. While they, too, are usually brief, they should be composed with skill and appreciative spirit.

Refusal to Serve

DEAR SIR:
    I will not be able to serve in the Canvass Sunday.
           Sincerely in Christ,

Such a letter is much too abrupt and too brief, and gives the impression of indifference.

Response to Invitation Received Too Late

DEAR DR. JONES:
    Your gracious invitation to attend the dedicatory services of the Union Avenue Christian Church reached my office while I was out of the city for two weeks, thus it was impossible for me to attend the dedicatory services of your new and renewed facilities. I regret this very much.
    I congratulate you and the church upon your splendid progress and your very significant service.
           Sincerely,[11]

In a response such as this, one senses, beyond the context of regret, the genuine tones of congratulation and interest.

Special Dinner

DEAR _____:
    Thank you for your thoughtfulness and kind invitation to attend the special dinner at Culver-Stockton College, Friday, October 9.

[11] Written by Dr. H. G. Harmon, President, Drake University, Des Moines. Used by permission.

I wish it were possible for us to attend, but our schedule precludes it this time. I hope it will be a satisfying evening and one which will come up to your expectations and hopes.

With appreciation for our friendship and with all good wishes, I am

Cordially,

Lectures to Ministers

DEAR MR. _____:

Thank you for your letter of October 8 and for your kind invitation to bring two lectures to the ministers of Indiana.

I would like to accept this invitation, but I find that I have a tentative commitment to preach a mission the week of March 1, which would preclude this. Otherwise, it would be a pleasant privilege. I hope you may ask me again.

With all good wishes, I am

Sincerely,

Investment Solicitation

DEAR MR. _____:

Thank you for your letter of February 8 and for the invitation to participate in the investment certificate program for your church.

I can appreciate your need, but we have just gone through this for our Disciples Council here in St. Louis and now would not be the propitious time to approach our people.

With all good wishes, I am

Sincerely,

RESIGNATION

It is not easy to resign. There is always the temptation to allow one's emotions to supersede his judgment and good taste. This is particularly true when one resigns under pressure. Considerable grace is necessary to sever one's professional or personal relationship with an institution, staff, or individual.

Associate Minister

DEAR DR. JONES:

It is not easy to write a letter of resignation as Associate Minister of the Union Avenue Christian Church. We have been made to feel from the very start that we were among friends. The church is blessed, most certainly, with a strong and loyal staff, as well as able and cooperative leadership in every department. This has not been an easy job, but a pleasant and challenging one.

My decision has not been brought about by any misunderstanding or any unsatisfactory conditions of any kind. Dr. Jones, you have known every step through which the decision has passed —in fact it goes back to our first conference in Nashville concerning my coming here. We agreed then that my tenure of service would not be of long duration. We discussed the plans of Mrs. Clayton and myself eventually going to Florida in the not too distant future.

Last July, the Central Church of Orlando, Florida, asked me to come there in September as their co-minister. I thought I should not leave here at that time. Later they came back about the possibility of my coming in November. I explained to them our program involving the Shepherding Plan and the Driskill Campaign and gave them the same answer. Then at Des Moines they again asked me to come. This time they said that if it was a question of salary, "let's talk about that." I explained to them that it was not salary, as they were offering me a thousand dollars per year more than my present salary. To this they replied that a committee had been appointed to see me, but if I did not accept, the committee was to contact another man. I considered the matter closed.

About a month after I got home I told you about this. Your reply was that I should not pass this up, for me to call them and see if the place had been filled and if it had not we would work out something. By the first of the year the Driskill program would be over and the Shepherding Plan completely organized and functioning. I called Dr. Carpenter and he said he hardly knew where the committee was, but would let me hear from them soon. On Friday night they reported my telephone call to the Board and voted to take it to the church. Both groups gave me a unanimous call to come and take up the work on January 1.

It is needless for me to say any more about it being hard to leave Union Avenue. I am not going among strangers, however.

The first two years we were in Florida we were members of this church. Dr. Carpenter was called to this church on my recommendation. Later he served three years on the Florida State Board while I was State Secretary. Two of the present deacons were deacons in Montgomery, Alabama, church during my ministry there.

The consideration given me by you in this change is just typical of the unselfish consideration which has been given me by the entire Staff and membership of the church. My short stay at Union Avenue has been most gratifying, and I want you and the church Staff and the church members with whom I have worked to know that I appreciate the genuine aid and cooperation and I shall always have a tender spot in my memory for the Union Avenue Christian Church.

Sincerely,[12]

An unusually kind and intimate letter, saturated with sincerity and affection.

Secretary

DEAR DR. JONES:

I would like to submit my resignation as Church Secretary, effective March 15, to accept a position with the _____.

The thirty-one years as a member of the staff of this church have meant much to me and have enriched my life. My work has given me deep satisfaction, and the happy relationships with those with whom I have worked will be difficult to sever. However, I look forward to the new opportunity with the _____ which is an important part of the brotherhood of the Disciples of Christ.

Of course I will continue to be an active member of this church and do all I can to support the program.

My best wishes go with the Church always.

Sincerely yours,[13]

The writer reveals herself to be the soul of integrity. Her continuing interest in the church is apparent.

[12] Written by T. Boyd Clayton, Associate Minister, Union Avenue Christian Church, St. Louis. Used by permission.
[13] Used by permission.

Minister Changing Churches

To the Members of _____:

A few weeks ago I stated from the pulpit that another great church of our brotherhood was in correspondence with me relative to my becoming its minister and that I would advise you of developments and of my decision. Since then, the invitation to become minister of _____ has been extended and I have accepted.

This opportunity to go to _____ presented me with the most difficult decision of my life. Much was involved. Earnestly we sought to know God's will in the matter. My relationship to the Kingdom, two fine congregations and the brotherhood, as well as the future welfare of our family were all so interrelated and interwoven that, believe me, it was an enervating experience.

The easier decision would have been for us to remain. . . . We like it here and you have been good to us. The more difficult one was to go to _____ for it is a larger, more demanding church in a teeming city. After agonizing over the situation, praying about it, and conferring with friends, we have chosen to give the best years of our lives to a metropolitan church that has decided to remain an inner-city witness.

In tendering my resignation as minister of _____, I wish to express profound gratitude for the privilege of shepherding this congregation. You have meant much to me and to my family. I shall always cherish the memories of our ministry together and remember you with thanksgiving and lingering love.

.   .   .   .

In all courtesy and sincerity, no disappointment nor disagreement with any one or with any group in the congregation dictated my resignation. Indeed, my regard for this Church is as high as ever and my heart genuinely warm.

Furthermore, lest there be suspicions and misunderstanding, insofar as I know, Dr. _____ had nothing to do with my call to _____ nor my leaving _____. Indeed, the _____ Church was in correspondence with your pastor long before our senior shepherd was asked to be their ad interim minister.

In compliance with our working agreement—namely that either party desirous of a change should grant the other a minimum of ninety days notice—I have every intention of fulfilling my contract and plan to continue, with your permission, through Easter. I want to be of every possible assistance and shall continue to serve you unreservedly during the remainder of my ministry here. I shall endeavor to leave the Church in the best possible condition for my successor.

When a pastor leaves a parish there is always a temptation for him to select or to influence in the selection of his successor. If desired, I stand ready to counsel with the Board and the Pulpit Committee on procedures in calling a minister, but I will not recommend a successor.

Long may _____ live to serve the needs of _____, to honor and to perpetuate the nobler concepts of the Disciples of Christ, and to glorify God in such a contagious affinity of faith and work that the world will believe.

_____ and _____ join me in wishing for you and this Church every conceivable good fortune and blessing.

Affectionately,

Minister Emeritus to a Resigning Colleague

DEAR CURTIS:

On the eve of your departure, I give you my renewed admiration, appreciation, and love. We have all spoken in a limited way of our indebtedness to you for your leadership, and your preaching, but it may be permitted me to speak intimately of what you have meant to me as the first pastor I have had since accepting a church in 1903. I thank you from my heart for your many thoughtful considerations, for your concern for me during my illness, for all the courtesies you have extended to us on our intermittent visits, and pray that it may be given to you in your new work to be such a friend and shepherd of many who will need you more than sometimes you may know.

If we could do anything for Sybil and the boys during these coming weeks, I trust they will feel free to call us and make us happy in the thought of some service to them.

May God continue his blessings to you, making you increasingly a good servant of Christ and His Church throughout the world.

Ever with love,[14]

[14] Written by Dr. Roger T. Nooe, Minister Ecumenical, Vine Street Christian Church, Nashville. Used by permission.

This is one of the cherished letters of my ministry. Dr. Nooe, Minister Ecumenical of Vine Street Christian Church, Nashville, and the first minister, to my knowledge so designated in Protestantism, was a source of real inspiration and joy during my ministry in the Athens of the South. This letter is the acme of genuine friendship.

9

Confidential, Difficult, and
Anonymous Letters

CONFIDENTIAL

There is a Latin proverb which says that confidence begets confidence. And so it should. Daniel Webster spoke from great depths of insight when he declared that men could not be catapulted into trust. Confidence is the product not of compulsion but of genuine character and growth. This is what William Pitt meant when he referred to confidence as "a plant of slow growth in an aged bosom. Youth is the season of crudity."

To be entrusted with a confidence is to be custodian of another's innermost thoughts, emotions, and aspirations. It is to be invited to live with another through periods of perplexity, crises, and victory. It is to be acquainted with the strengths and weaknesses of another, and to minister to his problems with utter tenderness and understanding. It is to possess what John Galsworthy called "breadth of heart." To share a confidence is to rise to Christ's levels of expectancy, affection, and compassion for others.

Few people live with more confidences than a minister. If he told all that he knew about the members of his congregation, he would be very unpopular, if not unemployed. The minister must train himself to be discreet in judgments, careful in pronouncements, and unvenal in the keeping of confidences. Almost daily, the min-

134

ister receives confidential letters ranging from marital problems to church secrets, from character references to medical reports, from psychopathic patients to political overtures.

The conscientious minister will not procrastinate in answering confidential mail. While he must be cautious, at the same time he must be sympathetic and sincere. Great care must be taken in composing such letters and the letter, as well as the envelope, should always be marked "Personal and Confidential." Such correspondence should be kept in a confidential file, available only to the minister and his secretary.

Although one could not, of course, publish confidential letters, the following replies to counseling situations may indicate possibilities in this area of correspondence.

Adopting a Child

MY DEAR _____ :

You were very kind to come in the other day and share with me your desire to adopt a child. My physician friend to whom I referred advises me that the "best agency according to our social service department is the _____ of _____." This agency in _____ is headed by _____. The main office is at _____ and the phone number is _____. It has an excellent reputation and attempts to place the infants as rapidly as possible so that the average adoption proceedings are carried out within one year. . . .

. . . .

I trust that this information will give you a start and I shall be anxious to know how you make out at _____. You might tell them that I suggested your coming and that I formerly served on the _____.

Please command me if I can be of additional service.

With all good wishes, I am

Sincerely,

A Minister Relocating

DEAR _____ :

Thank you for your letter of _____. Although I appreciate your confidence, I am somewhat reluctant to advise you in your decision. I had no idea that you were considering a change. But that is beside the point now.

It would seem to me that your basic decision is between general work and the pulpit. Naturally, I would like to see you try the preaching ministry, and for it to try you, but then you know better than I your capacities and desires.

As for the _____ I would, of course, be delighted to see you in the state. We have an excellent setup and one of the top secretaries of the brotherhood. You would do a good job. . . .

Please be assured of my help, irrespective of the direction in which you decide to turn. . . .

I just got back from a trip to the East where I saw _____ and _____. They are fine as are the other members of our family.

With all good wishes, I am

Cordially,

DIFFICULT

There is also an area of difficult situations wherein the writer must be candid, kind, and helpful. Though the minister may not always be able to accede to a request, his response must convey honor, empathy, and appreciation.

Divorce

MY DEAR MR. _____:

I have read carefully the decree of divorcement which you gave me Sunday.

I very much appreciate your spirit in the matter, and although I wish that I could conscientiously perform the ceremony . . . I think it would be far better for all concerned if you were married in the county in which the divorce was granted, provided this were the home county of your bride-to-be.

I trust you appreciate my position and realize that I am dealing with recorded facts as indicated in the enclosed document and not with personalities.

With every possible good wish and hoping that you will call by to see me when you are in town, I am

Sincerely,

The Question of Baptism

DEAR MR. _____:

It seems to me that you reached pretty far this time to find heresy in my writing, although I am always glad to hear from you. My comment on _____'s letter made no intimation whatsoever "that strict adherence to the doctrines of the Christian Church would be a return to Roman Catholic practice," as you say.

It must have been very obvious to the careful reader what my comment meant. It referred to the second paragraph of Mr. _____'s letter, not the first.

In other words, the Roman practice at Worms was exactly opposite the practice advocated at Corinth where the church was split up into four parts. Nothing was said at all about kicking out the ones who were wrong. Your remarks about my doctrine are true. I would not administer sprinkling, but I am a human being. Therefore, I could not advocate that anyone who disagrees with me should get out and join a denomination that agrees with him. You and I belong to the same church, although we have often disagreed, through the years. The last thing I would want would be for you to be in a different church because you disagreed with me. We are both human. The divine word of God may suffer in our hands, but we have to do the best we can with it.

With best regards, I remain

Cordially yours,[1]

Scathing Letters

Every public servant receives his share of letters from "crackpots," prisoners of prejudice and ignorance, who venture to tell him how to run his business or how to conduct the church, though these people have never made a success of anything, including the graces of charity. The minister should be very careful not to censure such incompetent writers nor to engage them in debate. For instance, here is a most critical letter:

[1] Written by Dr. Howard E. Short, Editor, *The Christian*, St. Louis. Used by permission.

To the Church Men:

I'm just wondering what has become of the old fashioned way of worship. Has our church been turned into a Methodist Church? All forms and fashions?

Why has the communion service been relegated to a hole in the wall? Why is it not out in front where it belongs? And why is it not taken before the sermon to prepare our hearts for the worship? Why all the long robes and red flashes?

Why don't we hear gospel sermons instead of a lot of stuff others say about social doings?

These are a few questions for the preachers and the Board. Please give it to them.

Yours very respectfully,
A Brother in Christ

While one seldom chooses to reply with silence, the above letter may qualify for such treatment.

Dear Dr. Jones:

Since answering your letter of May 5th and your statement of March 31st causes me to think more about both.

Before mailing this, I have consulted some other friends and members who advised me to take the steps I am about to take. As I told you previously I had not attended _____ in 8 weeks.

Of course you haven't missed me. Have you made any inquiry as to whether I was sick or anything else. No but when you want money you think to write me. So long as we have money for all your wants and give its different. Dr. Jones if this is religion I don't want it.

You have known ever since you came here that I am not by choice an alcoholic. Have you shown any desire to help me or any other unless they had money like some of them who are on the board and I can give you their names that are alcoholics.

I ask you to talk to my son, which you promised to do but if you did I have never heard of it.

Please read the first 3 verses 6 Chap of Galatians. What is the meaning of these verses? Other changes you have made since you came here I do not approve as well as many others. I hope you see fit to mention in your sermon Sunday what I said about your subject.

Yours truly,

Alcoholics are to be pitied and helped. It is most difficult to correspond with them.

ANONYMOUS

Generally speaking, an anonymous letter communicates destructive criticism. It is a vituperative method of unloading one's emotions and misinformation on another. More often than otherwise, it indicates lack of character and courage. One must condition himself to receiving such harangues, and though the recipient may think he knows the sender, the letter should be quietly filed and forgotten.

Reaction to a Book

Dear Dr. G. C. Jones:
Your latest book, *Youth Deserves to Know*, was very poorly written especially Chapter VI About Marriage. We do not agree with you about what you have to say about mixed marriages in the Catholic Church. May I be allowed to quote a phrase— "Catholics consider themselves to be the only true Church." Well, Sir, for your information, we do not consider it, but we know it. We are the one true Church. Our Church does not criticize or ridicule other so-called Christian Churches like yours and many others I have seen or heard of, but other so-called Christian Churches believe in ridiculing, criticizing making fun of and putting us on the spot continually. If you want to be a good writer you should obtain all the facts. There are a few good hints in the book but all in all it is not worth paper it is printed on. I think the book should be cancelled and be rewritten.
Do You Understand? ? ? I am sure we would not take the risk of being insulted, ridiculed, and made monkeys of again, by reading another of your so-called books.
Signed:
Two Girls who are Catholics

P.S. One of us are born of a Protestant parent who later converted to Catholicism.

Let it be said that the composer of this caustic letter writes a beautiful hand! But the letter reeks with prejudice and animosity. The sender displays behind her mask of anonymity the very characteristics which she would have it believed she deplores.

Church Choir

DEAR _____:

As a long time member of _____ I feel that I have a right to a suggestion for the improvement of the Church.

Our choir is getting so terrible that it almost makes you weep to listen to the funeral dirge they sing every Sunday.

I suggest we take some of the *nice sum* donated to us by a deceased member, and make an improvement in our music.

We need a soloist like other Churches and a good one, if we intend to keep on a par with others.

This is not only my opinion, but the consensus of opinion of a good many of our members.

Respectfully,
A MEMBER

The choir has been frequently referred to as the "War Department" of the church. This ineffective letter was obviously from a member who had not the courage nor the courtesy to speak to the minister of music or to the pastor about his complaints. As with the authors of many anonymous messages, he wants someone else to correct the faults and to pay the bills.

Chain-Letter Humor

Chain letters seem to move in cycles. They vary tremendously in intent and promised awards. Some of them are even humorous. Thank God for the saving grace of a sense of humor!

DEAR FRIEND:

This letter is started in hopes of bringing relief and satisfaction to disturbed preachers.

Unlike most chain letters, *this does not cost any money.* Simply send a copy of this to five of your preacher friends who are equally disgusted. Then bundle up your Education Director and send him to the man whose name is at the top of this list and add your name to the bottom of it.

When your name comes to the top of the list you will receive 15,625 Education Directors, and some of them will be "dandies."

Have faith— Don't break the chain—one preacher did and got his old associate back.

Sincerely,
A DISSATISFIED AND DISTURBED PREACHER

P.S. At the time I wrote this a friend of mine received 336 Education Directors. Today he is planning to begin shock treatments as soon as they can be arranged.

Private Crusades

DEAR SIR:

Perhaps your people have already thought about it before, but I am writing to you with the hope that the following suggestions will be taken up before them for sure.

That the Christian Church bend every effort toward the end that the sale of alcoholic beverages be stopped. It is my prayer that all churches, regardless of faith or creed do the same thing so that the accursed liquor traffic will be banished forever.

They give the excuse that they are afraid of the bootlegger. The Government of the U.S. should be ashamed of itself to say such a thing. They proved that they were not afraid of Germany and Japan. Why should they be afraid of bootleggers. The traffic in poison drugs is banned except one, and that is alcoholic beverage which is a poison habit forming drug which weakens the mind and poisons the body, according to science and actual proof.

Sugar and grains the main ingredients of liquors are needed for the war effort and food. It is past time that they should stop being wasted in the making of something that causes crime, suffering, poverty and death, not only to its users but to other innocent people as well.

Another suggestion is that you and your people see to it that the Bible is taught in every school, also the dangers and results which drinking intoxicants cause.

They say it is unconstitutional to have the Bible taught in school paid for by the taxpayers money. If so the Constitution should be amended, so that it will become a textbook in all schools, and be taught as a regular subject. It could be a voluntary subject, but all pupils and scholars would be given a chance to study it under proper guidance.

Some will think these things cannot be done, others will say they are unpopular, still others will say Oh! it is not worth while. It can be done and will be done if people will get behind the movement and ask God to help us through prayer to Him, having faith. Thus we will live up to the motto on our money, "in God We Trust." Let us not only trust Him but let us serve him everyday.

Please bring this before your church or see that it is brought before them in the forthcoming convention.

Yours truly

A BELIEVER IN JESUS CHRIST

A devoted person who felt that the ills of mankind would be solved if liquor traffic were abolished. Here again the minister must be gentle and brief in his reply.

Glorious Anonymity

Thank God all anonymity is not censorious. Many generous and devout souls prefer to remain anonymous in their deeds and letters. Every church has a sprinkling of anonymous saints. They are a wellspring of encouragement and comfort to the congregation and a fountain of unceasing joy to the minister.

MY DEAR _____:

I've always been one who liked to thank people who have helped and inspired me in one way or another. Since it is next to impossible to speak to you at any length after a service it has been on my mind to drop you a letter—and have put it off until now—and am doing it while the remembrance of your service today is still very warm in my heart and mind.

Having once been a preacher myself, I think I have a better appreciation and understanding of a service of worship and a minister's message than most people do. I have been worshipping in your church for some time, and though a Presbyterian, feel myself at home and inspired in your Church. I like the dignity of it—that being the Presbyterian in me, I suppose. Since I love good music, I thoroughly enjoy your choir, the high caliber of the hymns and the wonderful use of music in the communion service.

But most of all I believe I get my greatest enjoyment and blessing from your sermons. Every one I have heard has been fine. I know a minister is seldom able to keep his sermons always at the peak of perfection, but you may take it from me—yours are always excellent. I was telling someone the other day—you get beneath the surface of things—you are deep in your thinking and perception of human nature, but you are never over one's head. How close you get to the human heart and how close you bring it to God at the same time. The presence of the Lord is very real to me while you are preaching the Word. As far as I am concerned the compliment that was noted on your bulletin cover several weeks ago, to Phillips Brooks might well be applied to you. I do not say that as shallow flattery. I mean that from the heart. Your people should prize you highly.

I thought your sermon today was excellent—and though you believe in immersion in baptism, I was glad you conceded to the possibility of other modes. You know, of course, how Presbyterians feel. To me the mode is not important—that is not what saves a man, ultimately—but I would not argue the point with any man. I know people have their differences of opinion and that is their right and privilege. It is only when they begin to say, as you noted, that only by "my" way can you be saved, that I part company with them. One thing I will say of the Presbyterian Church, that she has never been guilty of such an attitude. At any rate, I thought your sermon was marvelous and as always an inspiration to me. I have needed much spiritual uplift during recent months. I might have found it in a church of my own denomination, but found it once in yours and have continued coming without having experienced, even once, disappointment.

I am only here in _____ for a while and will probably be leaving within a month or so, but meanwhile I hope to continue to worship with you and receive inspiration.

I do not think it is necessary to sign my name, but only to let you know you have the thanks of—

An Appreciative Friend

Dear _____:

The fine work that you do each day, other than what you are called upon to do for your congregation, has not gone unnoticed.

The many hours each day and each week that you take from some type of personal entertainment and devote toward making our community a better place in which to live will always be remembered and will be symbolical of you.

The example that you set by your thoughtful acts, your patient approach to problems that you must bear along with others, and your ever willing desire to help those that are less fortunate, is a most commendable trait. In short, you are one of the few ministers that I know who actually "practices what you preach."

This letter is anonymous in order that its sincerity cannot be doubted, and is for the sole purpose of letting you know that your presence among us is sincerely and deeply appreciated.

Most sincerely yours,

A Friend

10

Inquiries, Recommendations, Employment

There is always a premium on capable, consecrated personnel. Institutions and corporations have long since learned the value of sound personnel policies and relationships. No organization is stronger than its people.

Much is being said about unemployment in the United States. We sometimes forget that the vast majority of the unemployed are untrained, unlettered folk who, with their limited resources and skills, will find it increasingly difficult to secure and maintain regular employment in a highly technical and competitive society. This is one obvious price of automation. Progress superimposes its penalties. The constant maneuvering between management and labor, lobbyists and politicians, however regrettable and ridiculous it may be, is now an acceptable weapon of bargaining and employment.

Although the church is not, at the moment, encumbered by organized restrictions and demands of the market place, the mere fact that certain working conditions, standard practices, pay scale, and benefits exist, inevitably places the church in the competitive market for some of its workers. Paradoxically enough, the church is also a participant in this complex business of employment, for no single institution, no one person recommends more individuals for positions in a community than the church and its minister.

The search for capable and conscientious workers continues. Virtually every day the minister must reply to queries from prospective employers concerning an acquaintance or a member of his congregation. The pastor must be honest and at the same time helpful to all concerned. Letters of inquiry and recommendation are usually considered important by those requesting references. The minister should be prompt and articulate in such correspondence. His letter could be the determining factor in one's employment. It could also be very detrimental to the employer. The pastor should answer letters of inquiry concerning people and fill in confidential questionnaires carefully and accurately. Such correspondence is highly confidential, and to break this trust is all but unforgivable.

INQUIRIES

The minister receives a great variety of letters of inquiry. Here are a few:

DEAR _____:
Your name has been given by _____ of _____ as a reference. We are interested in learning as much as possible about him to see if he can be used in a pastorate in _____.
We will appreciate receiving from you a very frank description of the kind of person he is, the abilities and weaknesses he possesses, and the type of church that you feel he is best qualified to serve.
We thank you in advance for this information and assure you that it will be held in confidence by _____ and me.
Sincerely yours [1]

DEAR _____:
The Pulpit Committee of this church has obtained information schedules from the Office of Ministerial Services, on a number of men. Your name was listed as a reference on the Information Schedule of _____ and we will appreciate it if you will write us a letter concerning him.
We are seeking a senior minister to replace _____ who re-

[1] Written by the Associate Secretary of a State Missionary Society. Used by permission.

signed to become _____. Our church has _____ resident members and a budget of a little over _____; our World Outreach budget is about _____. Our building indebtedness is low, and we hope to be able to enlarge our Educational Facilities in the near future. We are located in a city of _____ which is the headquarters of two large _____ companies. Because the administration and research functions of these two companies are centered here, we have a high per capita education. Our church is quite liberal theologically, although it has members of all theological positions.

We will appreciate your giving us as frank an evaluation as possible, indicating both strong and weak points. We are interested in such factors as personality and personal characteristics (and those of his wife); ability to manage personal affairs; effectiveness as a leader in areas of membership development, evangelism, stewardship, missionary giving, and religious education; administrative ability; ability in pastoral counseling and pastoral calling.

At this state of our search we have not made direct contacts with any of the ministers we are considering as possibilities, and we do not know if Mr. _____ would be interested or available, or what salary he would require. If you have any information regarding this, it would be of interest to us.

Please be assured that we shall hold your reply in strict confidence.

Sincerely,[2]

DEAR _____:

We believe you can give us some helpful information concerning _____, now minister at the _____ at _____.

As secretary of our Pulpit Committee, I am writing to ask the favor of your frank evaluation of his work as a pastor, and as a preacher.

Instead of asking certain questions, I feel that by your own remarks concerning Mr. _____, you can give us a good idea of his background, his preparation for the ministry, his general ability and his record of service and leadership.

We shall especially appreciate your appraisal of his capacity to lead a church such as ours at _____. Our membership is _____ and our present total budget is nearly $_____.

[2] Written by the chairman of a pulpit committee.

I would appreciate your reply at your earliest convenience to
my home address below.

Yours very truly,

Searching for Personnel

Discovering and securing personnel is a delicate and time-
consuming task. The minister of the church may employ many
methods of discovering personnel. He will work through the official
channels of his communion and through counselors in the areas
where assistance is needed, will write personal letters, and in the
case of some employees will discreetly advertise.

My dear Mr. _____:

We are interested in securing a young man to join our staff
as director of youth and young adult work. You have been recommended and I am writing to ascertain your interest. If so, I would
appreciate receiving your biographical sketch and photograph.

With all good wishes, I am

Sincerely,

Dear _____:

Confidentially, I am seeking an able associate to help me
at _____. What would you think of _____? I realize he
is older than one would normally desire, but personally, I would
prefer a seasoned elderly man for a few years to a younger man
with less experience. I would appreciate your evaluation. Since I
am leaving tomorrow, if you could write me by the weekend, it
would be most helpful.

Thanking you and with all good wishes, I am

Cordially,

Application

It is generally agreed that the way for a minister not to receive a
call to a desired church is to apply for it. Such persons are seldom
considered. However, this is not true with all church personnel.
There is a definite place for the letter of application. Many ministers
prefer to create situations wherein a desired candidate or prospect
would need to reply by letter in order that his ability to communicate

effectively and accurately can be evaluated. As a matter of fact, two of the most efficient secretaries I have ever had were discovered through blind newspaper advertisements. Though this is time-consuming, the process pays dividends, for if the applicant cannot write a good letter, certainly she would not be a desirable secretary. The applicant who wrote the following letter was offered the job.

GENTLEMEN:

I am interested in the position of private secretary to a minister of a metropolitan church as advertised in the _____.

In lieu of a detailed resume, which it is my practice to present, and which I do not now enclose because of the blind advertisement, I should like to say that I am mature, experienced, and have a good religious background. I am Protestant, Methodist and have been widowed a short time.

Following are some of those who will recommend me: _____ School, where I was Secretary to [Chief Administrator] as well as being engaged in some teaching duties; _____ Company, where I carried on a special administrative work; _____ School, where I worked part time for a period of years before becoming employed full time. I have performed administrative work on special assignments at _____ University in the past for (well known educator and scientist) in the returning veterans' program, UNESCO and others.

My abilities run to public relations, I have been trained in journalism, I now edit my own church newspaper, have taught Sunday Church School, and for a number of years have read from memory for many groups at the entertainment and inspirational level.

As to office skills, I can operate any typewriter, electric or manual, adding machine, teletype, stencils. I take good dictation (Gregg) and transcribe well. I have taught typing. Added to this, I have categorized and instituted new files in many offices in _____ (city) such as schools, public and private, businesses, and for individuals. I worked with _____ (nationally known editor) on special assignment in connection with _____ (name of editor) work on _____ (national magazine).

If the above is of interest, I shall be glad to come in for an interview, bringing with me a detailed record, complete with references and recommendations. My telephone number is _____.

Very sincerely yours,

RECOMMENDATIONS

It is in this area that the minister must exercise utmost caution and integrity. Much is at stake. Filling in tedious questionnaires and letters of recommendation call for thought and care.

DEAR _____:

I am in receipt of the questionnaire concerning _____. I found it to be rather difficult inasmuch as information requested in certain categories is beyond my knowledge.

Suffice it to say I have known _____ since he was a young boy in _____. In fact he used to keep our children for us. He is a fine young man, well oriented in the church. I have had a feeling through the years that he needed more drive and dynamic forcefulness in leading people. However, I am advised by those who are much closer to him than I that he has matured in the last few years, is a very acceptable preacher, and is a hard worker. On the basis of what I know, I would certainly commend him to you.

With all good wishes, I am
Sincerely,

MY DEAR _____:

I have your good letter of April 7 concerning _____ and am happy you are aiding her to secure a position, and I can say, confidentially, that I would recommend her without any reservation.

_____ was a victim of circumstances due to some personality problems in _____. There are no irregularities involved, and it was one of those problems that occur occasionally in human relationships. I think she would do a good job and I most heartily recommend her.

Very cordially yours,

DEAR MR. _____:

I am enclosing herewith the confidential report as per your request on _____.

I can never be too sure as to equity and justice in filling in such a complicated questionnaire because all people are different and thus do not always fit an academic pattern. Therefore I take the liberty of volunteering the following paragraph:

I have known _____ for a number of years, in fact we were in Yale together. He is an able, consecrated, and aggressive minister. He is unusually well-trained and sensitive to things of the spirit. He has a lovely family. In my judgment, you would be most fortunate to secure him.

With all good wishes, I am
Cordially,

Dear _____:

I am in receipt of your letter relative to _____.

I first met _____ when we were in _____. He was then a student at Vanderbilt and a very good one. He was active in the total life and witness of our church. In fact, I think it was during this period he began to seriously consider the ministry. We had several conferences about it.

I think _____ is a splendid young man. He comes of a good family, his father being one of our ministers. I think he would be a credit to the ministry and to _____. I commend him to you.

With all good wishes, I am
Sincerely,[3]

My dear Dr. _____:

_____, an active member of _____ Church, and an unusually fine young man, has indicated an interest in interning in _____ Hospital. Whereas, to be sure, I am not familiar with your standards or procedures of selectivity, I am happy to commend _____ to you as a capable, attractive man of real character. His wife _____ is equally fine.

_____ will graduate from _____ University School of Medicine in June and he will then be ready to commence his internship. I have every reason to believe he will be a credit to the medical profession. Feel free to command me for any further information.

Thanking you for considering _____ and with all good wishes, I am
Sincerely,

Many persons do not care to write "To Whom It May Concern" letters. However, they have their place. Here is an example:

---

[3] Addressed to the dean of a prominent theological seminary.

To Whom It May Concern:

This letter is to certify that _____ of _____ was cook for _____ Church for approximately a year. We found him to be clean, dependable and most cooperative.

Please call for any additional information.

Sincerely,

EMPLOYMENT

After discovering the person (or persons) one feels would fit into the staff, he then must proceed to describe in general terms responsibilities and working relationships.

MY DEAR CURTIS:

At the request of Mr. _____, Chairman of our Pulpit Supply Committee, I am writing you the action of our Council and Cabinet, meeting jointly last night at the church.

You were unanimously invited to become associate minister of _____ at a salary of _____ with _____ for your car, expenses of moving, and also the continuation of your _____ fund. This invitation is extended on a five-year basis, with a proviso that by mutual consent the relationship can be severed on a ninety-day basis.

It gives me great pleasure to transmit this action to you and to say to you and your dear wife that we hope very much that you will give us a favorable answer. Also it is good of you to say that you could make that answer within a week, for time is precious these days it seems to me above all days.

We enjoyed so much your visit with us. I only regret that I could not have been with you Sunday night. I hear splendid reports of your address and you had an enthusiastic reception, I assure you.

With all good wishes, and hoping to have a favorable report shortly, I am

Most sincerely yours,[4]

DEAR _____:

Thank you for your letter of _____.

[4] Written by the late Dr. Edgar DeWitt Jones, Central Woodward Christian Church, Detroit. Used by permission.

I have given considerable thought to our conversations relative to the possibility of your becoming my associate, and definitely feel that you are the man I would like to recommend.

Would you be interested in the position herewith described and the compensation mentioned?

(1) As Associate Minister, you would carry responsibility for membership conservation, cultivation, evangelism and integration of new members. You would be expected, of course, to assist me in every possible way, such as sharing in the morning service, upholding my hands and efforts and being responsible for the welfare of the church in my absence. Your major responsibility, however, would be in the general areas of membership cultivation and evangelism.

(2) You would have secretarial assistance.

(3) We would expect you to attend our conventions whenever possible and would so provide in our budget.

(4) You would have a month's vacation at a time most suitable in the light of the entire staff and the program of the church.

(5) We would suggest a starting salary of _____ per annum, pension dues, plus a car replacement fund, which would accumulate at the rate of _____ per month, and a discretionary allowance of a like amount per month. We would propose to evaluate your work at the end of the year and if it is generally acceptable, as I am sure it would be, then you could expect an increase in salary.

(6) The church would bear your moving expenses. _____, I very much want you to come to _____. I feel that you are capable of rendering a lasting service to the church, and you may be assured of my cooperation and, I believe that of the church, in making any minor adjustments that would make you and Mrs. _____ happy.

You are correct in assuming that it is more expensive to live in _____ than your present community. I have conferred with several men who are in a position to know relative values and rentals and the highest quotation I have received on an apartment approximating your needs, as I understand them, was _____. If you will permit me to offer this word of counsel, I think your wife had a good idea in suggesting that you rent a furnished place for a while, which would enable you to look leisurely and carefully for a more suitable and permanent place.

Trusting that this tentative proposal will meet with your

favor and acceptance, and looking forward to hearing from you,
with all good wishes, I am
                          Cordially,

Confirmation of Agreements

No matter what the nature of employment or how many conferences are held and general agreements reached, it is *always*
wise to confirm in writing the proposals which were set forth and
agreements made. Because of this, some letters of confirmation are
necessarily long and tedious, but this is the time to clarify situations, declare intentions, and arrive at mutually acceptable procedures. This kind of communication is not a letter in the ordinary
sense: it is a contractual document which governs conditions of employment and continuing work.

DEAR _____:
        Since our previous communication with you, our _____
Committee has made an extensive survey of pastoral personnel
and is now ready to proceed with the matter of selecting a pastor
for the _____ Church.
        The Committee has authorized me to communicate further
with you with reference to your interest in the pastorate, your
availability, the question of salary and associated matters, such
as the manse, expense . . .
        We stand ready to exchange views and information as to all
present policies, practices, program and the administrative organization now obtaining at _____ Church.
        We shall be pleased to hear from you at your earliest con-
venience.
                          Yours truly,[5]

DEAR MR. _____:
        Your letter of _____, relative to my becoming pastor of
_____ has been thoughtfully read and its contents prayerfully
considered.
        After due deliberation, I am writing to express my conclusions
and requests. If they merit acceptance by the Board and congregation, my answer will be in the affirmative. As I said, in our first

[5] Written by president of a church board.

conference, if the Board and congregation are willing to pay the price in prayer, in work, in service, in money, for an ever-expanding program as I envision it and as we further develop it together, I should be honored to become your minister.

(1) If I become your pastor, I must be linguistically and theologically free. I will not, of course, expect the congregation to accept everything I say, but I must be free to say it.

(2) It is understood that the policy of inclusive membership will be retained, receiving into active fellowship, and with full status, without immersion, Christians from other communions who may, through their own choice or otherwise, transfer to _____. Individuals who confess Christ for the first time and present themselves for membership will be immersed.

(3) Regarding the changing neighborhood, the ultimate composition of which no one can prophesy, be it understood that I should want our church to follow the finest in Christian traditions and practices; and should the future dictate an inter-racial church, it must not deplete nor divide our fellowship.

(4) It occurs to me that the lush days of growth at _____ are over. This being true, the future ministry of the church cannot be evaluated solely by statistics. We must seek to expand and deepen spiritual concerns. Our growth from within must match if not exceed our growth from without. Hard as we would work to gain new members, it could not be considered a statistical ministry.

(5) In so far as I am concerned, the program of _____ will continue to be that of our brotherhood. The annual goals of the church will be our proportionate share of those of the brotherhood. In addition, the church must accentuate its community service and at the same time become a greater metropolitan church.

(6) I have been a bit concerned over the stewardship life of the church. Should I become your minister, I will constantly challenge you to be better stewards in every area of Christian living and witnessing and will forever press for a larger budget— not only for ourselves but for the work of the Kingdom throughout the world.

(7) Regarding the staff—it is my conviction that a church program, in large measure, coincides with the policies and visions of a congregation, plus a sufficiently diversified and dedicated staff to implement dreams and needs. I should want to work toward the following staff:

a. An Administrative Assistant, whose task would be to calendarize the program, to keep committees moving, attend to matters of business, keep records and reports, and channel responsibilities within administrative areas. I should hope this person would be a layman. He, as well as other staff members, would be directly responsible to the minister.

b. I would suggest that the lady who has been the minister's private secretary become the front office secretary. She would be invaluable in the area of public relations and general information. (This move should be made prior to the new minister's arrival.)

c. I should want an able associate who would strengthen my hands at every point but who would also have specific responsibilities for membership cultivation and development. In this area, I should want us to study our membership throughout the city most carefully, organizing and putting into operation what I choose to call "the shepherding plan," which we have used at _____ most effectively. If these conclusions are acceptable, I should like to be given the "green light" immediately to secure an associate, for, ideally, we should arrive there about the same time in order that we might facilitate acquaintance studies and program planning. (Incidentally, I know the man I would like to have. I believe he would be interested. He has had considerable experience and is about my age.)

d. In addition, I should want a Minister of Education. It is my understanding that your present Director's contract will not be renewed. I should expect you to notify her of your decision in this matter, making it clear that it was not that of the new minister. (This procedure should apply to any other staff member whom you wish to replace.)

e. I would need, of course, a very efficient private secretary who would look after my personal calendar, correspondence, assist in the preparation of sermons, and in my writing.

f. As far as I know, the music personnel is satisfactory.

g. The present hostess, chef, and sextons are acceptable.

h. I would be content with the other members of the staff. As the new staff emerges and the work expands, I know consideration will be given to adequate secretarial aid and other assistance throughout the organization.

(8) I should hope that the staff thus envisioned could be fully realized within two years' time. However, I would have to insist

on having my Associate, my Minister (or Director) of Education, and my private secretary join me immediately upon arrival or as soon thereafter as they are attainable. Otherwise, I would be stymied and our program would get off to an inauspicious beginning.

(9) You will appreciate the spirit of this reminder—Mrs. _____ [wife] is not to be regarded in any way as a member of the church staff. Whereas you will find her a very diligent and able worker, she prefers to strengthen the church in inconspicuous ways. She has never held an office in any church that we have served and we would not want to break that precedent.

(10) You will appreciate the fact that I look upon my writing as a definite part of my ministry. I should hope, therefore, that no criticism would arise as to the amount of time I spend in this extension of the church. I would, of course, be as considerate as possible.

(11) In this regard, I would expect the church to afford me travel experiences. I should hope that it would be more or less periodic inasmuch as I feel a minister of a great city church, such as yours, needs to be a voice and nothing so enables him to become and remain that voice as the tuition of the years plus fruitful travel.

(12) I should want to be free to accept speaking engagements across the country. I would use discretion in this matter, accepting those which would not interfere too much with the program of _____, as well as those that would attract me and where I would feel I could make a worthy contribution.

(13) As I have said before, the _____'s need an ample house. We now occupy the equivalent of a nine-room manse, plus attic and basement and we use every bit of it. It is essential that the house be roomy, for in addition to our large family, we enjoy entertaining. We feel that four bedrooms would be a minimum —five would be better—as well as two baths, an ample den with adequate shelving for books, and as much yard as possible. It is understood that the maintenance and insurance of the house will be carried by the church, whereas the minister will pay for the utilities. We would consider it a real courtesy to have the privilege of exploring and evaluating the proposed manse, in light of our needs, before the purchase.

(14) Salary as mentioned in "a" under 3 of your letter of _____ is satisfactory, though I would expect increases for myself as well as for the staff. I would, of course, continue in the Pension Fund.

(15) The automobile replacement fund as shown in "b" under 3 is entirely satisfactory.

(16) It is perfectly agreeable with me for convention and conference expenses to be carried in the annual budget since this figure will fluctuate from year to year. However, I would expect the church to send _____ (my wife) with me to our conventions.

(17) The vacation of six weeks (adjustable by consent) is generous.

(18) Arrangements outlined for the Associate Pastor, as indicated in "a" under 4 of your letter are agreeable, though I think we would have to anticipate an increase for him at the end of the first year.

(19) As I see it, it would be unwise and entirely unfair to _____ for me to terminate my ministry here until the fulfillment of my contract—namely, ninety days from the time of resignation. And my resignation will not be announced until this agreement, or a mutually acceptable one, has been officially confirmed by your congregation. Assuming acceptance, I could begin in _____, soon after _____. This would necessitate arrangements being made for Mrs. _____ (and family) to stay on here through the remainder of the school year. Meanwhile, I would assume responsibilities at _____ trying to assemble the staff and get organized.

(20) You were kind to agree to bear the moving expenses of our household goods and equipment to _____. I know that you would see that it was adequately packed and covered by insurance. I am warning you—we have an awful lot of "stuff!"

Mr. _____, I hope you will not think that I have been too didactic. I have tried to summarize our conferences, as I remember them, as well as to set forth the general working conditions under which I would be happy. I realize that I have been brutally frank. However, if the existing courtship—between church and preacher—is to culminate in a happy and lasting marriage, then we must understand each other.

Should these considerations be acceptable and should they be confirmed by your people, then I will be happy to accept the invitation to become pastor of _____. It goes without saying that in accepting so great a responsibility, I would bring to the charge my undivided loyalties and total consecration, for I should want us not only to maintain the present greatness of _____, but also to increase it.

Permit me to reiterate my sincere appreciation for the confidence you have expressed. I am gentled by it. Now, my decision is your decision.

Sincerely,

After agreements have been reached, letters of declaration and confirmation exchanged and accepted, it is sometimes desirable to have a general contractual statement signed by proper church officials and the minister, to protect all parties concerned. In the event of sudden and unforeseeable changes in the leadership of the church, such a document is invaluable. The statement need not be long, but should be definitive.

DEAR _____:

For reference and guidance of future Official Boards and officers of said Boards, we state herein the mutual understandings and agreements which constitute the contractual relationship between the Official Board of _____ and you, as its Minister.

Our letter to you dated _____, with item 4b amended as indicated, and item 5 added, together with your letter of reply dated _____, show and confirm the vital elements of mutual commitments. Copies of these letters are attached and are part and parcel of this contract. Your letter to us and a copy of our letter to you will remain in the permanent office files of _____ Church. The modified item 4b referred to above is amended to the effect that the Associate Minister would have a _____'s vacation and car allowances as well as other allowances indicated in item 4b. Item 5 added immediately following the item 4 concerns the requirement of 90 days notice of change in contract with you or your associate. I believe you have now such an arrangement with _____ Church.

Wherein these two letters are at slight variance with reference to timing and staff provisions, it is understood that your views would prevail as indicated in your letter.

It is understood that both the Church and the Minister are committed to a program of working, giving and serving, to the end that your proposed program of expansion and staff development may be realized and _____ can and will become the great church you and we envision.

In witness of mutual good faith and purpose, the undersigned affixed their signatures.

_____
Minister

_____

_____

_____

Church Officers, 19___

11

Letters That Never Grow Old

Ralph Waldo Emerson was severely shaken by the death of his eleven-year-old son. He wrote in his journal, January 30, 1842, "The sun went up in the morning sky, but the landscape was dishonored by his loss, for this boy in whose remembrance I have both slept and waked so often, decorated for me the morning star, the evening cloud and all the particulars of daily life." After the boy was buried in Concord Cemetery, Emerson went home and wrote these lines:

> As God lives,
> The excellent becomes the permanent.

And so it does! This is the essence of our faith. Some things in life are too glorious and precious to die. Literature has its own immortality. Great letters never die.

SOLDIERS AND STATESMEN

War correspondence is unique. Military men, frequently regarded as callous and stern, have left through their letters significant insights into their philosophies, thoughts, and wills. One is sometimes amazed at the sentiment and tenderness expressed. With the surrender of General Lee at Appomattox, April 9, 1865, the military campaign ended and the Confederacy was dissolved. It was a trying time, emotionally and economically. In closing his reports, Lieutenant-General Joseph Wheeler, distinguished cavalryman, wrote this magnificent message to his men.

April 29, 1865

GALLANT COMRADES:

You have fought your battles; your task is done. During a four years' struggle for liberty, you have exhibited courage, fortitude and devotion; you are the sole victors of more than two hundred severely contested fields; you have participated in more than a thousand successful conflicts of arms. You are heroes, veterans, patriots. The bones of your comrades mark battlefields upon the soil of Kentucky, Tennessee, Virginia, North Carolina, South Carolina, Georgia, Alabama, Mississippi; you have done all that human exertion could accomplish. In bidding you adieu, I desire to tender my thanks for your gallantry in battle, your fortitude under suffering, and your devotion at all times to the holy cause you have done so much to maintain. I desire also to express my gratitude for the kind feeling you have seen fit to extend toward myself, and to invoke upon you the blessings of our heavenly Father, to whom we must always look for support in the hour of distress.

Brethren in the cause of freedom, comrades in arms, I bid you farewell.

J. WHEELER [1]

Apparently George Washington had many misgivings regarding the leadership of the Revolutionary forces. He did not seek the post. His dedication to the cause and his personal dignity are clearly evident in this letter to his wife.

[1] Published under the Auspices of Wheeler's Confederate Cavalry Association and edited by W. C. Dodson, Historian, *Campaigns of Wheeler and His Cavalry* (Atlanta: Hudgins Publishing Company, 1899), pp. 359–360.

PHILADELPHIA
18 June, 1775

MY DEAREST:

I am now set down to write to you on a subject which fills me with inexpressible concern, and this concern is greatly aggravated and increased when I reflect upon the uneasiness I know it will give you. It has been determined in Congress, that the whole army raised for the defence of the American cause shall be put under my care, and that it is necessary for me to proceed immediately to Boston to take upon me the command of it.

You may believe me, my dear Patsy, when I assure you in the most solemn manner, that, so far from seeking this appointment, I have used every endeavor in my power to avoid it, not only from my unwillingness to part with you and the family, but from a consciousness of its being a trust too great for my capacity, and that I should enjoy more real happiness in one month with you at home, than I have the most distant prospect of finding abroad, if my stay were to be seven times seven years. But as it has been a kind of destiny that has thrown me upon this service, I shall hope that my undertaking it is designed to answer some good purpose. You might, and I suppose you did perceive, from the tenor of my letters, that I was apprehensive I could not avoid this appointment, as I did not pretend to intimate when I should return. That was the case. It was utterly out of my power to refuse this appointment without exposing my character to such censures as would have reflected dishonor upon myself and given pain to my friends. This, I am sure, could not, and ought not, to be pleasing to you, and must have lessened me considerably in my own esteem. I shall rely, therefore, confidently on that Providence which has heretofore preserved and been bountiful to me, not doubting but that I shall return safe to you in the fall. I shall feel no pain from the toil or the danger of the campaign; my unhappiness will flow from the uneasiness I know you will feel from being left alone. I therefore beg that you will summon your whole fortitude, and pass your time as agreeably as possible. Nothing will give me so much sincere satisfaction as to hear this, and to hear it from your own pen. My earnest and ardent desire is, that you would pursue any plan that is most likely to produce content and a tolerable degree of tranquillity; as it must add greatly to my uneasy feelings to hear that you are dissatisfied or complaining at what I really could not avoid.

As life is always uncertain, and common prudence dictates to every man the necessity of settling his temporal concerns while it is in his power, and while the mind is calm and undisturbed, I have, since I came to this place (for I had not time to do it before I left home), got Colonel Pendleton to draft a will for me, by the directions I gave him, which I will now enclose. The provision made for you in case of my death, will, I hope, be agreeable.

I shall add nothing more, as I have several letters to write, but to desire that you will remember me to your friends, and to assure you that I am, with the most unfeigned regard, my dear Patsy, your affectionate, &c.[2]

Horace Greeley, editor of the *New York Tribune,* was considered one of America's greatest journalists. However, his brilliance and enthusiasm frequently combined to catapult him into rash statements. He was impatient with the progress of the Civil War. On August 19, 1862, he published a sentimental piece entitled, "Prayer of Twenty Millions of People," in which he declared that Lincoln was too much under the influence of slave power. Lincoln's reply is an excellent example of his gift for handling people and for communicating.

> Executive Mansion, WASHINGTON
> August 22, 1862

DEAR SIR:

I have just read yours of the 19th instant, addressed to myself through the *New York Tribune.* If there be in it any statements or assumptions of fact which I may know to be erroneous, I do not now and here controvert them. If there be in it any inferences which I may believe to be falsely drawn, I do not now and here argue against them. If there be perceptible in it an impatient and dictatorial tone, I waive it, in deference to an old friend whose heart I have always supposed to be right.

As to the policy I "seem to be pursuing" as you say, I have not meant to leave anyone in doubt.

I would save the Union. I would save it in the shortest way under the Constitution. The sooner the national authority can be restored, the nearer the Union will be "the Union as it was." If there be those who would not save the Union unless they could

[2] From *Speeches and Letters, George Washington* (New York: Little Leather Library Corporation), pp. 50–53.

at the same time save slavery, I do not agree with them. If there be those who would not save the Union unless they could at the same time destroy slavery, I do not agree with them. My paramount object in this struggle is to save the Union, and is not either to save or to destroy slavery. If I could save the Union without freeing any slave, I would do it; and if I could save it by freeing all the slaves, I would do it; and if I could save it by freeing some and leaving others alone, I would also do that. What I do about slavery and the colored race, I do because I believe it helps to save the Union; and what I forbear, I forbear because I do not believe it would help to save the Union. I shall do less whenever I shall believe that what I am doing hurts the cause; and I shall do more whenever I shall believe doing more will help the cause. I shall try to correct errors when shown to be errors, and I shall adopt new views so fast as they shall appear to be true views.

I have here stated my purpose according to my view of official duty, and I intend no modification of my oft-expressed personal wish that all men everywhere could be free.

Yours,

A. LINCOLN [3]

The late Franklin Delano Roosevelt had a remarkable capacity for correspondence. He wrote with skill and finesse. He corresponded with a vast cross section of people, ranging from children to celebrities, from kings and queens to war lords and peacemakers. There was a disarming informality and intimacy in his style. His deft touch is brilliantly illustrated in his letter to Premier Joseph Stalin.

My dear Mr. Stalin:

I am sending this personal note to you by the hands of my old friend, Joseph E. Davies. It relates solely to one subject which I think it is easier for us to talk over through a mutual friend. Mr. Litvinov is the only other person with whom I have talked about it.

I want to get away from the difficulties of large Staff conferences or the red tape of diplomatic conversations. Therefore, the simplest and most practical method that I can think of would be

[3] Charles W. Moore (ed.), *Lincoln Addresses and Letters* (New York: American Book Company, 1914), p. 137. Used by permission.

an informal and completely simple visit for a few days between you and me.

I fully appreciate the desirability for you to stay in daily touch with your military operations; I also find it inadvisable to be away from Washington more than a short time. There are two sides to the problem. The first relates to timing. There is always the possibility that the historic Russian defense, followed by taking the offensive, may cause a crack-up in Germany next Winter. In such a case we must be prepared for the many next steps. We are none of us prepared today. Therefore, it is my belief that you and I ought to meet this Summer.

The second problem is where to meet. Africa is almost out of the question in Summer and Khartum is British territory. Iceland I do not like because for both you and me it involves rather difficult flights, and, in addition, would make it, frankly, difficult not to invite Prime Minister Churchill at the same time.

Therefore, I suggest that we could meet either on your side or my side of Bering Straits. Such a point would be about three days from Washington and I think about two days from Moscow if the weather is good. That means that you could always get back to Moscow in two days in an emergency.

It is my thought that neither of us would want to bring any staff. I would be accompanied by Harry Hopkins, an interpreter and a stenographer—and that you and I would talk very informally and get what we call "a meeting of the minds." I do not believe that any official agreements or declarations are in the least bit necessary.

You and I would, of course, talk over the military and naval situation, but I think we can both do that without Staffs being present.

Mr. Davies has no knowledge of our military affairs nor of the post-war plans of this Government, and I am sending him to you for the sole purpose of talking over our meeting.

I greatly hope that our forces will be in complete control of Tunisia by the end of May, and Churchill and I next week will be working on the second phase of the offensive.

Our estimates of the situation are that Germany will deliver an all-out attack on you this Summer, and my Staff think it will be directed against the middle of your line.

You are doing a grand job! Good luck!

Always sincerely,[4]

[4] Elliott Roosevelt, *F.D.R., His Personal Letters, Vol. II* (New York: Duell, Sloan & Pearce, 1950), pp. 1422–1423. Copyright 1950 by Elliott Roosevelt. Used by permission.

BETWEEN GENERALS

Here is an interesting exchange between Field Marshall Montgomery and General Dwight D. Eisenhower. Montgomery is reported to have been very unorthodox in following recognized military procedures and communications. His letter glistens with masculine grace.

DEAR IKE:

Now that we have all signed in Berlin I suppose we shall soon begin to run our own affairs. I would like, before this happens, to say what a privilege and an honor it has been to serve under you. I owe much to your wise guidance and kindly forbearance. I know my own faults very well and I do not suppose I am an easy subordinate; I like to go my own way.

But you have kept me on the rails in difficult and stormy times, and have taught me much.

For all this I am very grateful. And I thank you for all you have done for me.

Your very devoted friend,
MONTY [5]

General Eisenhower replied:

Your own high place among military leaders of your country is firmly fixed, and it has never been easy for me to disagree with what I knew to be your real convictions. But it will always be a great privilege to bear evidence to the fact that whenever decision was made, regardless of your personal opinion, your loyalty and efficiency in execution were to be counted upon with certainty.[6]

Few men of the English-speaking world communicate as eloquently as Sir Winston L. Spencer Churchill. His letters, like his speeches, are redolent with simplicity and strength. His words, like the manifold notes of a mighty organ, flood the mind with music and beauty. In this letter to King George VI of England may be found the inimitable Churchill characteristics of directness and dignity.

[5] Dwight D. Eisenhower, *Crusade in Europe* (New York: Doubleday & Company, Inc., 1948), pp. 286–287. Used by permission.
[6] *Ibid.*

January 5, 1941

SIR:

I am honoured by Your Majesty's most gracious letter. The kindness with which Your Majesty and the Queen have treated me since I became First Lord and still more since I became Prime Minister has been a continuous source of strength and encouragement during the vicissitudes of this fierce struggle for life. I have already served Your Majesty's father and grandfather for a good many years as a Minister of the Crown, and my father and grandfather served Queen Victoria, but Your Majesty's treatment of me has been intimate and generous to a degree that I had never deemed possible.

Indeed, Sir, we have passed through days and weeks as trying and as momentous as any in the history of the English Monarchy, and even now there stretches before us a long, forbidding road. I have been greatly cheered by our weekly luncheons in poor old bomb-battered Buckingham Palace, and to feel that in Your Majesty and the Queen there flames the spirit that will never be daunted by peril nor wearied by unrelenting toil. This war has drawn the Throne and the people more closely together than was ever before recorded, and Your Majesties are more beloved by all classes and conditions than any of the princes of the past. I am indeed proud that it should have fallen to my lot and duty to stand at Your Majesty's side as First Minister in such a climax of the British story, and it is not without good and sure hope and confidence in the future that I sign myself "on Bardia Day," when the gallant Australians are gathering another twenty thousand Italians prisoners,

Your Majesty's faithful and devoted servant and subject,

WINSTON S. CHURCHILL.[7]

AUTHORS, PUBLISHERS, AND CRITICS

Louisa May Alcott, product of a remarkable family and a distinguished storyteller, reveals in this brief letter her exuberance and gratitude in receiving an unexpected royalty check from her publisher.

[7] Winston S. Churchill, *Their Finest Hour* (Boston: Houghton Mifflin Company, 1949), pp. 627–628. Used by permission.

BOSTON, December 28, 1869

Many thanks for the check which made my Christmas an un-usually merry one.

After toiling so many years along the uphill road,—always a hard one to women writers,—it is peculiarly gratifying to me to find the way growing easier at last, with pleasant little surprises blossoming on either side, and the rough places made smooth by the courtesy and kindness of those who have proved them-selves friends as well as publishers.

With best wishes for the coming year,

I am yours truly,

L. M. ALCOTT [8]

Not everyone is adept at handling criticism, especially through correspondence. In the November, 1885, issue of *Time* (a periodical now extinct), William Archer, "a very clever fellow," published a critical article on Robert Louis Stevenson. He referred to the courageous Scotsman as "a full-blooded fox hunter" whose philosophy of life would not survive the rigors of illness and inconvenience. This is Stevenson's reply:

Skerryvore, BOURNEMOUTH
November 1, 1885

DEAR MR. ARCHER:

You will see that I had already had a sight of your article and what were my thoughts.

One thing in your letter puzzles me. Are you, too, not in the witness-box? And if you are, why take a wilfully false hypothesis? If you knew I was a chronic invalid, why say that my philosophy was unsuitable to such a case? My call for facts is not so general as yours, but an essential fact should not be put the other way about.

The fact is, consciously or not, you doubt my honesty; you think I am making faces, and at heart disbelieve my utterances. And this I am disposed to think must spring from your not having had enough of pain, sorrow, and trouble in your existence. It is easy to have too much; easy also or possible to have too little; enough is required that a man may appreciate what elements of

[8] Ednah D. Cheney, (ed.), *Louisa May Alcott, Her Life, Letters, and Journals* (Boston: Little, Brown & Company, 1907), p. 203. Used by permission.

consolation and joy there are in everything but absolutely over-powering physical pain or disgrace, and how in almost all circum-stances the human soul can play a fair part. You fear life, I fancy, on the principle of the hand of little employment. But per-haps my hypothesis is as unlike the truth as the one you chose. Well, if it be so, if you have had trials, sickness, the approach of death, the alienation of friends, poverty at the heels, and have not felt your soul turn round upon these things and spurn them under—you must be very differently made from me, and I ear-nestly believe from the majority of men. But at least you are in the right to wonder and complain.

To "say all"? Stay here. All at once? That would require a word from the pen of Gargantua. We say each particular thing as it comes up, and "with that sort of emphasis that for the time there seems to be no other." Words will not otherwise serve us; no, nor even Shakespeare, who could not have put *As You Like It* and *Timon* into one without ruinous loss both of emphasis and substance. Is it quite fair then to keep your face so steadily on my most light-hearted works, and then say I recognise no evil? Yet in the paper on Burns, for instance, I show myself alive to some sorts of evil. But then, perhaps, they are not your sorts.

And again: "to say all"? All: yes. Everything: no. The task were endless, the effect nil. But my all, in such a vast field as this of life, is what interests me, what stands out, what takes on it-self a presence for my imagination or makes a figure in that little tricky abbreviation which is the best that my reason can conceive. That I must treat, or I shall be fooling with my readers. That, and not the all of some one else.

And here we come to the division: not only do I believe that literature should give joy, but I see a universe, I suppose, eternally different from yours; a solemn, a terrible, but a very joyous and noble universe, where suffering is not at least wantonly inflicted, though it falls with dispassionate partiality, but where it may be and generally is nobly borne; where, above all (this I believe; probably you don't: I think he may, with cancer), *any brave man may make out* a life which shall be happy for himself, and, by so being, beneficent to those about him. And if he fails, why should I hear him weeping? I mean if I fail, why should I weep? Why should *you* hear *me*? Then to me morals, the conscience, the af-fections, and the passions are, I will own frankly and sweepingly, so infinitely more important than the other parts of life, that I conceive men rather triflers who become immersed in the latter;

and I will always think the man who keeps his lip stiff, and makes "a happy fireside clime," and carries a pleasant face about to friends and neighbours, infinitely greater (in the abstract) than an atrabilious Shakespeare or a backbiting Kant or Darwin. No offence to any of these gentlemen, two of whom probably (one for certain) came up to my standard.

And now enough said; it were hard if a poor man could not criticise another without having so much ink shed against him. But I shall still regret you should have written on an hypothesis you knew to be untenable, and that you should thus have made your paper, for those who do not know me, essentially unfair. The rich, fox-hunting squire speaks with one voice; the sick man of letters with another.

Yours very truly,

ROBERT LOUIS STEVENSON [9]

The very mention of Lord Byron evokes an adjective in appreciation. He was a voluminous writer and correspondent. One is impressed by his grace and politeness as seen in his letter to the great German poet Goethe.

ILLUSTRIOUS SIR:

I cannot thank you as you ought to be thanked for the lines which my young friend, Mr. Sterling, sent me of yours; and it would but ill become me to pretend to exchange verses with him who, for fifty years, has been the undisputed sovereign of European literature. You must therefore accept my most sincere acknowledgements in prose—and in hasty prose too; for I am at present on my voyage to Greece once more, and surrounded by hurry and bustle, which hardly allow a moment even to gratitude and admiration to express themselves.

I sailed from Genoa some days ago, was driven back by a gale of wind, and have since sailed again and arrived here, "Leghorn," this morning, to receive on board some Greek passengers for their struggling country.

Here also I found your lines and Mr. Sterling's letter: and I would not have had a more favourable omen, a more agreeable surprise, than a word of Goethe, written by his own hand.

I am returning to Greece, to see if I can be of any little use

[9] Sidney Colvin, *The Letters of Robert Louis Stevenson to His Family and Friends,* Vol. 1 (London: Methuen & Co., 1899), pp. 371–373. Used by permission of The Society of Authors.

there: if ever I come back I will pay a visit to Weimar, to offer
the sincere homage of one of the many millions of your admirers.
I have the honour to be, ever and most respectfully, y[our]
Obliged adm[irer] and se[rvant],
NOEL BYRON [10]

ARTIST AND ARTISAN

Michelangelo is remembered as one of the most renowned in
a cluster of brilliant Florentine artists. Born poor, he fought the
battle of poverty throughout his life. At one time in his career he
slept with three working men in one bed. Despite parental
opposition, early he determined to be an artist. Most of his life
was spent in and around Rome. He excelled in architecture, engineering, sculpture, painting, and poetry. Surprisingly enough, he
was a sharp financier, as illustrated in his dealings with Pope
Julius II.

FLORENCE, May 2, 1506

MAESTRO GULIANO, Architect to the Pope:
Guliano, I learn from a letter sent by you that the Pope was
angry at my departure, that he is willing to place the money at
my disposal and to carry out what was agreed upon between us;
also, that I am to come back and fear nothing.
As far as my departure is concerned, the truth is that on Holy
Saturday I heard the Pope, speaking at table with a jeweler and
the Master of the Ceremonies, say that he did not want to spend
another baiocco on stones, whether small or large, which surprised me very much. However, before I set out, I asked him
for some of the money required for the continuance of my work.
His Holiness replied that I was to come back again on Monday;
and I went on Monday, and on Tuesday, and on Wednesday, and
on Thursday—as His Holiness saw. At last, on the Friday morning,
I was turned out, that is to say, I was driven away; and the person
who turned me away said he knew who I was, but that such
were his orders. Thereupon, having heard those words on the
Saturday and seeing them afterwards put into execution, I lost

[10] Jacques Barzun (ed.), *The Selected Letters of Lord Byron* (New York:
Grosset & Dunlap, 1953), pp. 248–249. Used by permission of John Murray.

all hope. But this alone was not the whole reason for my departure. There was also another cause, but I do not wish to write about it; enough that it made me think that, if I were to remain in Rome, my own tomb would be prepared before that of the Pope. This is the reason for my sudden departure.

Now you write me on behalf of the Pope, and in similar manner you will read this letter to the Pope. Give His Holiness to understand . . . that if he really wishes to have this tomb erected it would be well for him not to vex me as to where the work is to be done, provided that within the agreed period of years it be erected in St. Peter's, on the site he shall choose, and that it be a beautiful work as I have promised; for I am persuaded that it will be a work without equal in all the world if it be carried out. [It was the tomb of Julius II.]

If His Holiness wishes to proceed, let him deposit the said money here in Florence with a person whose name I will communicate to you. . . . With regard to the aforesaid money and work, I will bind myself in any way His Holiness may direct, and I will furnish whatever security here in Florence he may require. Let it be what it may, I will give him full security, even though it be the whole of Florence. There is yet one thing I have to add: it is this, that the said work could not possibly be done for the price in Rome, but it could be done here because of the many conveniences which are available, such as could not be had in Rome. . . . I beg of you to let me have an answer, and quickly. I have nothing further to add.

Your MICHEL ANGELO,
Sculptor, in Florence [11]

Paul Revere, the silversmith, was courageous in his communications. He was also proud of his ability to cast great bells. The following letter indicates his impatience with the Farmington Academy for their delinquency in paying for a church bell.

July 1810

MR. SUPPLY BELCHER:

We think it extrodinary that Gentlemen of your Respectability will not so far respect your own credit as not to notice in anyway our letters to you: You know you have a Bell, you know

[11] Curtis Gentry, *Fifty Famous Letters of History* (New York: Thomas Y. Crowell Company, 1930), pp. 60–62. Used by permission.

who it was purchased of, who purchased it & the terms it was purchased upon and hear that Bell every Sabbath call you to the House of God & you all know it is not paid for. What are we to think of the Gentlemen who composed the Trustees of Farmington Academy?" [12]

Bon-Voyage

It is considerate to write colleagues and friends before they leave for important assignments.

In response to a call for help, John Wesley sent Richard Wright and Francis Asbury to America in 1771. While Asbury became the Wesley of America, Wright's contribution was apparently small. George Shadford, a man of gracious temperament and remarkable dedication, went to America in 1773. Here is Wesley's letter of embarkation and farewell.

March, 1773

DEAR GEORGE:

The time is arrived for you to embark for America. You must go down to Bristol, where you will meet with Thomas Rankin, Captain Webb and his wife.

I let you loose, George, on the great continent of America. Publish your message in the open face of the sun and do all the good you can.

I am, dear George,
Yours affectionately,[13]

Clever and Humorous

One usually thinks of Benjamin Franklin as a quiet businessman and scientist who had high standards for himself and expected others to be so disciplined. However, students of Franklin know that he was also a man of ready wit and humor. There is a legendary claim that the committee appointed to draft the Declaration of

[12] Esther Forbes, *Paul Revere, The World He Lived In* (Boston: Houghton Mifflin Company, 1942), p. 374. Used by permission.

[13] George Eayrs, *Letters of John Wesley*, A Selection of Important and New Letters with Introductions and Biographical Notes (London, New York, Toronto: Hodder & Stoughton, Ltd., 1915), p. 244. Used by permission.

Independence preferred Jefferson to Franklin because they feared
he would get in at least one joke!

To the Marquis de Lafayette

PASSY, September 17, 1782

DEAR SIR:

I continue to suffer from this cruel Gout; But in the midst of
my Pain the News of Madame de la Fayette's safe Delivery, and
your Acquisition of a Daughter gives me Pleasure.

In naming our Children, I think you do well to begin with
the most antient State. And as we cannot have too many of so
good a Race, I hope you and Madame de la Fayette will go thro'
the Thirteen. But as that may be in the common way too severe
a Task for her delicate Frame, and Children of Seven Months
may become as Strong as those of Nine I consent to the Abridge-
ment of Two Months for each; and I wish her to spend the Twenty-
six Months so gained, in perfect Ease, Health and Pleasure.

While you are proceeding, I hope our States will some of them
new-name themselves. Miss Virginia, Miss Carolina, and Miss
Georgiana will sound prettily enough for the Girls; but Massachusetts and Connecticut, are too harsh even for the Boys, unless they were to be Savages.

That God may bless you in the Event of this Day as in every
other, prays

Your affectionate Friend and Servant

B. FRANKLIN [14]

EXECUTIVE COURAGE

President Wilson was an ill man during the latter months of his
administration. Politicians pestered him and the press chastised him.
Concern mounted as to what steps should be taken to execute the
proper executive duties of the government. Facing such an emergency, Secretary of State Robert Lansing took it upon himself to
assemble the Cabinet to discuss matters of State. Upon hearing of

[14] Leonard W. Labaree and Whitfield J. Bell, Jr. (eds.), *Mr. Franklin, A
Selection from His Personal Letters* (New Haven: Yale University Press, 1956),
p. 54. Used by permission of Yale University Press and the University of Pennsylvania.

this unauthorized action, President Wilson wrote the following letter:

The White House

WASHINGTON, February 7, 1920

MY DEAR MR. SECRETARY:

Is it true, as I have been told, that during my illness you have frequently called the heads of the executive departments of the Government into conference? If it is, I feel it my duty to call your attention to considerations which I do not care to dwell upon until I learn from you yourself that this is the fact.

Under our constitutional law and practice, as developed hitherto, no one but the President has the right to summon the heads of the executive departments into conference, and no one but the President and the Congress has the right to ask their views or the views of any one of them on any public question.

I take this matter up with you because in the development of every constitutional system, custom and precedent are of the most serious consequence, and I think we will all agree in desiring not to lead in any wrong direction. I have therefore taken the liberty of writing you to ask this question, and I am sure you will be glad to answer.

I am happy to learn from your recent note to Mrs. Wilson that your strength is returning.

Cordially and sincerely yours,

WOODROW WILSON [15]

Mr. Lansing replied that he did not consider assembling the Cabinet a breach of loyalty and offered to resign. President Wilson, disappointed with the Secretary's explanation, accepted Lansing's letter of resignation.

A NEW PRESIDENT WRITES HOME

Few citizens realized the gravity and implications of President Roosevelt's lingering illness. His was an arduous and enervating administration. He died April 12, 1945. Shortly after Mr. Truman had taken the oath of office as President of the United States, he wrote this wonderfully intimate letter to his mother and sister.

[15] Curtis Gentry, *Fifty Famous Letters of History* (New York: Thomas Y. Crowell Company, 1930), pp. 178–179. Used by permission.

April 1945

DEAR MAMA AND MARY:

Well I have had the most momentous and the most trying time anyone could possibly have, since Thursday, April 12th.

Maybe you'd like to know just what happened. We'd had a long, drawn out debate in the Senate and finally came to an agreement for a recess at 5 P.M. until Friday, Apr. 13th.

When I went back to my office, a call from Sam Rayburn, Speaker of the House, was awaiting me. Sam wanted me to come over to the House side of the Capitol and talk with him about policy and procedure and, as Alice in Wonderland would say, "shoes and ships and sealing wax and things. . . ."

But—as soon as I came into the room Sam told me that Steve Early, the President's confidential press secretary, wanted to talk to me. I called the White House, and Steve told me to come to the White House "as quickly and as quietly" as I could. Well I told Sam I had to go to the White House on a special call and that he should say nothing about it.

I ran all the way to my office in the Senate by way of the unfrequented corridors in the Capitol, told my office force that I'd been summoned to the White House and to say nothing about it. . . .

When I arrived at the Pennsylvania entrance to the most famous house in America, a couple of ushers met me . . . and then took me up to Mrs. Roosevelt's study on the second floor.

She and Mrs. Boettiger, her daughter, and her husband, the Lt. Col., and Steve Early were there. Mrs. Roosevelt put her arm on my shoulder and said, "Harry, the President is dead."

It was the only time in my life, I think, that I ever felt as if I'd had a real shock. I had hurried to the White House to see the President, and when I arrived, I found I was the President. No one in the history of our country ever had it happen to him just that way.

. . . We waited for Bess and Margaret to arrive. We then had to scurry around and find a Bible for me to put my hand upon to take the oath. They finally found one. If I'd known what was afoot, I'd have used Grandpa Truman's Bible, which was in my office bookcase.

You of course know from the papers what happened and what has happened since.

Saturday afternoon, the White House funeral; Sunday morning the burial at Hyde Park, today my speech to Congress.

This afternoon we moved to this house, diagonally across the street (Penn Ave.) from the White House, until the Roosevelts had time to move out of the White House. We tried staying at the apartment, but it wouldn't work. I can't move without at least ten Secret Service men and twenty policemen. People who lived in our apartment couldn't get in and out without a pass. So—we moved out with suitcases. Our furniture is still there and will be for some time. . . . But I've paid the rent for this month and will pay for another month if they don't get the old White House redecorated by that time.

My greatest trial was today when I addressed the Congress. It seemed to go over all right from the ovation I received. Things have gone so well that I'm almost as scared as I was Thursday when Mrs. R. told me what had happened. Maybe it will come out all right.

Soon as we get settled in the White House you'll both be here to visit us. Lots of love from your very much worried son and bro.

HARRY [16]

CELEBRITIES AND CHILDREN

On September 21, 1897, Francis P. Church, editor of the *New York Sun*, received this remarkable letter:

DEAR EDITOR:
I am eight years old. Some of my little friends say there is no Santa Claus. Papa says, "if you see it in 'The Sun' it's so." Please tell me the truth, is there a Santa Claus?
VIRGINIA HANLON

Here is the wise and kind editor's reply:

Virginia, your little friends are wrong. They have been affected by the skepticism of a skeptical age. They do not believe except they see. They think that nothing can be which is not comprehensible by their little minds. All minds, Virginia, whether they be men's or children's, are little. In this great universe of ours, man is a mere insect, an ant, in his intellect, as compared with the boundless worth about him, as measured by the in-

---

[16] Harry S. Truman, *Memoirs, Vol. I, Years of Decisions* (New York: Doubleday & Co., Inc., 1955), pp. 43-44. Copyright 1955 by Time, Inc. Used by permission.

telligence capable of grasping the whole of truth and knowledge.

Yes, Virginia, there is a Santa Claus. He exists as certainly as love and generosity and devotion exist, and you know that they abound and give to your life its highest beauty and joy. Alas! how dreary would be the world if there were no Santa Claus! There would be no childlike faith, then, no poetry, no romance to make tolerable this existence. We should have no enjoyment, except in sense and sight. The eternal light with which childhood fills the world would be extinguished.

Not believe in Santa Claus! You might as well not believe in fairies! You might get your papa to hire men to watch in all the chimneys on Christmas Eve to catch Santa Claus, but even if they did not see Santa Claus coming down, what would that prove? Nobody sees Santa Claus, but that is no sign that there is no Santa Claus. The most real things in the world are those that neither children nor men can see. Did you ever see fairies dancing on the lawn? Of course not, but that's no proof that they are not there. Nobody can conceive or imagine all the wonders there are unseen and unseeable in the world.

You tear apart the baby's rattle and see what makes the noise inside, but there is a veil covering the unseen world which not the strongest man, nor even the united strength of all the strongest men that ever lived, could tear apart. Only faith, fancy, poetry, love, romance, can push aside that curtain and view and picture the supernal beauty and glory beyond. Is it all real? Ah, Virginia, in all this world there is nothing else real and abiding.

No Santa Claus! Thank God he lives, and he lives forever. A thousand years from now, Virginia, nay, ten times ten thousand years from now, he will continue to make glad the heart of childhood.[17]

As a child Helen Keller wrote many letters. One of her letters received this response from Dr. Oliver Wendell Holmes, the poet.

BEVERLY FARMS, MASS.
August 1, 1890

MY DEAR LITTLE FRIEND HELEN:

I received your welcome letter several days ago, but I have so much writing to do that I am apt to make my letters wait a good while before they get answered.

It gratifies me very much to find that you remember me so

[17] Reprinted by permission of the *New York World-Telegram and Sun*.

kindly. Your letter is charming, and I am greatly pleased with it. I rejoice to know that you are well and happy. I am very much delighted to hear of your new acquisition—that "you talk with your mouth" as well as your fingers. What a curious thing *speech* is! The tongue is so serviceable a member (taking all sorts of shapes, just as is wanted), the teeth, the lips, the roof of the mouth all ready to help, and so heap up the sound of the voice into the solid bits which we call consonants, and make room for the curiously shaped breathings which we call vowels! You have studied all this, I don't doubt, since you have practised vocal speaking.

I am surprised at the mastery of language which your letter shows. It almost makes me think the world would get along as well without seeing and hearing as with them. Perhaps people would be better in a great many ways, for they could not fight as they do now. Just think of an army of blind people, with guns and cannon! Think of the poor drummers! Of what use would they and their drumsticks be? You are spared the pain of many sights and sounds, which you are only too happy in escaping. Then think how much kindness you are sure of as long as you live. Everybody will feel an interest in dear little Helen; everybody will want to do something for her; and if she becomes an ancient gray-haired woman, she is still sure of being thoughtfully cared for.

Your parents and friends must take great satisfaction in your progress. It does great credit, not only to you, but to your instructors, who have so broken down the walls that seemed to shut you in, that now your outlook seems more bright and cheerful than that of many seeing and hearing children.

Good-by, dear little Helen! With every kind wish from your friend,

OLIVER WENDELL HOLMES [18]

MEMORABLE MISSIONARY

Dr. Thomas A. Dooley, famed young medical missionary to Laos, died in Memorial Hospital, New York, January 18, 1961. In six brief years he made a permanent impression on all who love people and serve the church. From his hospital bed in Hong Kong, December

[18] Elizabeth Colson and Anna Gansevoort Chittenden (collectors), *Children's Letters* (New York: Hinds, Hayden & Eldredge, Inc., 1905), pp. 37–38.

2, 1960, just forty-seven days before his death, he wrote this incomparable letter to the Reverend Theodore M. Hesburgh, President of Notre Dame University.

HONG KONG, December 2, 1960

DEAR FATHER HESBURGH,

They've got me down. Flat on the back . . . with plaster, sand bags and hot water bottles. It took the last three instruments to do it however. I've contrived a way of pumping the bed up a bit so that, with a long reach, I can get to my typewriter . . . my mind . . . my brain . . . my fingers.

Two things prompt this note to you, sir. The first is that whenever my cancer acts up . . . and it is certainly "acting up" now, I turn inward a bit. Less do I think of my hospitals around the world, or of 94 doctors, fund raising and the like. More do I think of one divine Doctor, and my own personal fund of grace. Is it enough?

It has become pretty definite that the cancer has spread to the lumbar vertebrae, accounting for all the back problems over the last two months. I have monstrous phantoms . . . as all men do. But I try to exorcise them with all the fury of the middle ages. And inside and outside the wind blows.

But when the time comes, like now, then the storm around me does not matter. The winds within me do not matter. Nothing human or earthly can touch me. A wilder storm of peace gathers in my heart. What seems unpossessable I can possess. What seems unfathomable, I fathom. What is unutterable, I can utter. Because I can pray. I can communicate. How do people endure anything on earth if they cannot have God?

I realize the external symbols that surround one when he prays are not important. The stark wooden cross on an altar of boxes in Haiphong with a tortured priest . . . the magnificence of the Sacred Heart Berrini Altar . . . they are essentially the same. Both are symbols. It is the Something else there that counts.

But just now . . . and just so many times, how I long for the Grotto. Away from the Grotto Dooley just prays. But at the Grotto, especially now when there must be snow everywhere and the lake is ice glass and that triangular fountain on the left is frozen solid and all the priests are bundled in their too-large too-long old black coats and the students wear snow boots . . . if I could go to the Grotto now then I think I could sing inside. I could be full of faith and poetry and loveliness and know more beauty, tenderness and compassion. This is soggy sentimentalism I know. Cold prayers from a hospital bed are just as pleasing to God as more youthful prayers from a Grotto on the lid of night.

But like telling a mother in labor, "It's okay, millions have endured the labor pains and survived happy . . . you will, too." It's consoling . . . but doesn't lessen the pain. Accordingly, knowing prayers from here are just as good as from the Grotto doesn't lessen my gnawing, yearning passion to be there.

I don't mean to ramble. Yes, I do.

The second reason I write to you just now is that I have in front of me the *Notre Dame Alumnus* of September 1960. And herein is a story. This is a Chinese hospital run by a Chinese division of the Sisters of Charity (I think). Though my doctors are British the hospital is as Chinese as Shark's Fin Soup. Every orderly, corpsman, nurse and nun know of my work in Asia, and each has taken it upon themselves to personally "give" to the man they feel has given to their Asia. As a consequence, I'm a bit smothered in tender, loving care.

With a triumphant smile this morning one of the nuns brought me some American magazines (which are limp with age and which I must hold horizontal above my head to read . . .). An old *National Geographic,* two older *Times,* and that unfortunate edition *Life* . . . and with these, a copy of the *Notre Dame Alumnus.* How did it ever get here?

So Father Hesburgh, Notre Dame is twice on my mind . . . and always in my heart. That Grotto is the rock to which my life is anchored. Do the students ever appreciate what they have, while they have it? I know I never did. Spent most of my time being angry at the clergy at school . . . 10 P.M. bed check, absurd for a 19 year old veteran, etc etc etc.

Won't take any more of your time, did just want to communicate for a moment, and again offer my thanks to my beloved Notre Dame. Though I lack a certain buoyancy in my bones just now, I lack none in my spirit. I must return to the states very soon, and I hope to sneak into that Grotto . . . before the snow has melted.

My best wishes to the students, regards to the faculty, and respect to you.

Very sincerely,
TOM DOOLEY [19]

[19] Used by permission of the Reverend Theodore M. Hesburgh, C.S.C., President, Notre Dame University.

12

Family Correspondence

Back in the nineteenth century, Henry Drummond, bright young Scotsman with phenomenal scientific promise, entered Edinburgh University at the age of fifteen. However, Moody and Sankey, American evangelistic preaching-singing team, caused a shift in Drummond's professional plans. Later he wrote his enduring book, *The Greatest Thing in the World.* "Love," he said, "should be the supreme thing—because it is going to last; because in the nature of things, it is an Eternal Life."

The greatest business in the world is not steel, gas, oil, electronics, space-pioneering equipment, nor agriculture, but the growing of children! What we do about them will determine the validity of our days and the nature of our destiny. The family exists to make visible and intensive God's love. The family is a miniature church seeking to live out the dimensions of its faith.

As carbohydrates, proteins, minerals, and other basic food ingredients combine to produce physical stamina and health, so do faith, forgiveness, and love unite to produce psychological and spiritual maturity. The intrinsic strength of the family is essential to our culture and religious stability. The family is the fundamental unit of society. It is the genesis of things holy and hazardous.

The American home is under fierce attack. Once it was as strong

183

as the log cabins that housed its members. Physically, technically, socially the visible home has undergone a tremendous change. It is a compact rest camp for those who return intermittently through the day and night to replenish their strength and sharpen their strategy for the bruising business of living.

This does not mean that spirit and faith have been relegated to closets marked "heirlooms," but it does suggest the increasing difficulty experienced by the modern family in discovering and maintaining a meaningful dialogue with God and one another. Even the Communists are aware of the deterioration of the American home. They gloat over our high divorce rate and general delinquency. They seem to think that because American women control most of the money, this is an indication that the role of the American male is inferior and disappearing. If their attack has any validity at all, it should cause us to re-examine the stoutness of the American home.

Many parents approaching what is termed "success" forget that to experience true happiness and satisfaction the child needs the parent and the parent needs the child. Love is not always what we think it is. Although it is centered in emotions and feelings, one's reactions and attitudes toward members of the family, as well as the community at large, grow or diminish in proportion to concern and cultivation. Love is not only acknowledging something deep within. It is accompanying someone in the way of life. Love is not only the articulation of feeling toward a member of the opposite sex or toward a member of one's family; it is also faith in another. Love is an active, reciprocal relationship. Paradoxically enough, the one who loves the most—not the loved—feels best and usually acts the best.

When children or other members of the family leave home for brief or prolonged periods of time, those remaining should demonstrate continuing concern and love through correspondence. Parents particularly should continue to communicate their feelings and hopes for their children through frequent letters. The parent who does not write to his child periodically cannot censure him for irresponsibility. Moreover, because of emotional stresses, the perspective of a parent, and the lack of opportunity for conversation, a parent can frequently communicate more clearly and intimately through correspondence. Ralph Waldo Emerson recognized the exemplary art of letter writing when he said in *Life:*

> The tongue is prone to lose the way,
> Not so the pen, for in a letter
> We have not better things to say,
> But surely say them better.

TO ONE'S WIFE

Approaching Death

By virtue of their unique relationship and responsibility, parents are afforded rare opportunities to write definitive personal letters to their children. Moreover, husband and wife are privileged to chronicle their love and concern for each other. I have often thought that it must require great courage and faith to live quietly with an incurable illness. Among the papers of a friend, an officer of our church, was found a letter to his wife. He wrote it following a very discouraging conference with his doctor. The letter was written April 18, 1956. Four years later he died.

My Dearest:

I am writing to tell you some things that I may not have the opportunity to say to you in person.

Yesterday I called on Dr. _____ and he was most discouraging. He told me that the results of treatments had not been what they had hoped and that I might have to have more surgery. Further, that he couldn't say my case was hopeless, but he certainly didn't offer any encouragement. I left his office "walking in a fog" for a while, wondering how I would be able to conceal my concern from you, _____ [name], when I arrived home. You had "that virus" that day. I believe I did hide my feelings pretty well.

I've done a lot of thinking since I learned I had this malignancy, and it is surprising how faith and trust have developed.

As is human, I don't want to leave this earth yet. (I guess we never do.) But honestly, I'm not afraid to die, and I do not say that lightly. No one is more conscious of his shortcomings than I, but I have tried to live according to God's will as I see it to be, and I confidently believe He has reserved a place for me. Actually, with all the good things that have come to me here, I shouldn't expect Heaven, too, but I know that God will deal justly with my soul.

Believe me when I say that by far my greatest concern is in leaving you. You have been my life for a long time, and I'm not in the habit of taking long trips without you. I'm shedding tears at the thought of leaving you because I love you more than you will ever know. But you know well that God will always be with you here, and it won't be long before we are together again, and what a joyous meeting that will be.

. . . .

Yes, I'm going to see a lot of people I haven't seen for a long time, including my father and mother and yours. I'll tell them all how wonderful you have been to all of us, and thank them for giving you to me. They, too, will be happy when I tell them that you are truly prepared to "come on up" whenever the good Lord sees fit to call you (and this He will surely do).

Now, you are going to be sad about my going on this journey, although I should like to hope that you wouldn't be. Dear one, you can be pretty miserable if you permit yourself to indulge in self-pity, but with God's help (and you know you can have that if you but ask for it) you can continue to contribute to and receive a lot from life here. Please maintain your interest in many things. This thing of parting temporarily is just a natural thing and a part of God's plan that we not remain on this earth forever, so why be sad about it?

. . . .

What a wonderful thing faith is! His love and promises mean more than anything in this world! What a dismal place this would be without them. Now these are not just thoughts I have only because of the circumstance, because I've always known them, and they have carried me through some pretty rough spots. Naturally I am more appreciative of them right now than ever before.

. . . .

Now I won't even pretend that I'm not excited and a little bit frightened in anticipating this journey. You know I'm always that way even before vacation trips. But I'm not bitter, for I have had the privilege of enjoying you all much longer than some husbands and fathers have with their loved ones. I've prayed hard that "this cup might pass from me" but also that "Thy will be done; not mine." All is in God's hands and all is well!

May the Good Lord always bless, keep and protect you—I'll see you later.

With great love,[1]

Before Surgery

Every minister is familiar with people who face illness, surgery, and extended travel without adequately sharing with their family and friends the state of their affairs. Complications and needless confusion are often regrettable premiums. Like writing a will, this kind of letter does not shorten one's days. Before hospitalization a few years ago, a minister wrote the same letter to two of his closest friends, one an attorney, the other a businessman, reacquainting them with certain aspects of his affairs and soliciting their cooperation in the guidance of his family.

August 25, 1956

MY DEAR _____:

Inasmuch as I am facing surgery Monday, August 27, and not knowing, of course, the outcome, I am writing this letter soliciting your cooperation and assistance should I not recover.

My insurance papers, pension plan and my will, together with a few securities, are in our lockbox at the _____ [name of bank]. _____ [name of wife], of course, knows everything about our business, though she may need assistance.

I believe with judicious handling, my insurance and investments would see the children through school. In this same lockbox is also a copy of my father's will, which includes his desires with regard to our farm in _____ [state]. Whereas I would regret it being necessary to sell the farm, thus removing it from a long family tradition of ownership, should it become necessary for _____ [name of wife] and the children's security, please work out proper arrangements with my sister _____ [name and address].

. . . .

[1] Used by permission.

I would not, of course, insist that _____ [name of wife] live at any given place, for many factors would have to be considered, though my judgment is the children would be much happier in the South. Furthermore, it would not cost as much to live. We have a lot of friends in _____ [name of town] and with our college there, it might afford advantages for schooling.

. . . .

Should I not recover, though I have every reason to believe I will, please do not permit sentiment to upset our little financial structure. I should not want an elaborate funeral. At this point, you would probably have to intervene, for some morticians have a way of exploiting emotions. I would want the interment to be in the family cemetery at _____ [name of town].

Whatever you can do to assist _____ [name of wife] and the children, knowing of my affairs and general desires will be appreciated.

With gratitude for our continuing friendship, I am
Most cordially,

P.S. _____ (wife's name) has a copy of this and other letters.

TO ONE'S SON

Sir Walter Scott was a remarkable man. He was a cripple from childhood who suffered intermittent illnesses throughout his life; he was never an impressive student; nevertheless he was both a gifted storyteller and a prolific writer. In variety and swiftness of writing he is without peer in the English-speaking world. Think of a man having more than sixty-four book titles—and many of them volumes! He wrote twelve volumes of poetry. His *Life of Napoleon* is in nine volumes. In addition, he edited eighteen sets of books and published numerous articles. One of his driving motivations to continue writing even after he was physically impaired was to pay debts incurred by a dishonest partner. Here was a man acquainted with sorrow, calamity, and poor health, yet busy and troubled as he was, a faithful correspondent. Here is one of his letters to his not-too-energetic son Charles, a student at Oxford.

EDINBURGH, 1st December 1824

MY DEAR CHARLES:

I write chiefly at present to say that with every wish to yield to whatever suits your comfort, I do not think it advisable that you should leave Oxford in the short Christmas vacation, as you propose in a letter to Sophia. Nothing suffers so much by interruption as a course of study; it is in fact just stopping the stone while it is running down hill, and giving yourself all the trouble of putting it again in motion, after it has lost the impulse which it had acquired. I am aware you propose to read in Wales, but as the only object of your leaving college would be to find amusement, I rather fear that to that amusement study is in much danger of being postponed. You will meet with many men, and these by no means such as can be termed indolent or dissipated, who will conceive their business at college well done if they can go creditably through the ordinary studies. This may do very well for men of independent fortune, or who have a direct entree into some profitable branch of business, or are assured from family connection of preferment in some profession. But *you*, my dear Charles, must be *distinguished;* it will not do to be moderate. I could have got you a good appointment in India, where you might have had plenty of field sports and made money in due time, but on your affording me proofs when under Mr. Williams, that you were both willing and able to acquire knowledge, I was readily induced to change your destination. God knows if I have chosen for the best, but this I am certain, that you, like every youth of sufficiently quick talent, have the matter much in your own power. Solitude and ennui you must endure as others have before you, and there is this advantage in both, that they make study a resource instead of a duty. The greatest scholars always have been formed in situations where there was least temptation to dissipation,—I do not mean that which is mischievous and criminal, but the mere amusements, in themselves indifferent or even laudable, which withdraw the mind from serious duty. I beg you therefore to remain *inter silvas academi,* although they are at the present season both lonely and leafless. We shall think of you with regret at Christmas, but we will be comforted with thinking that you are collecting in your solitary chambers the means of making yourself an honour to us all, and are paying an apprentice fee to knowledge and distinction. . . .[2]

[2] *Familiar Letters of Sir Walter Scott* (Edinburgh: David Douglas, 1894), Vol. II, pp. 222–224.

Before Important Event

During his senior year in _____ University, a minister's son was recommended for the Rockefeller Brothers Theological Fellowship. This relatively new program, designed to discover and interest young men in the Christian ministry, grew out of a concern for augmenting the ministry with capable leadership. Furthermore, it was believed that many worthy candidates for the ministry did not consider this profession, for fear they would not qualify or, once having committed themselves, could not gracefully change. When it was learned that this young man was in the finals of this carefully selected group of students across the country, his father wrote:

DEAR _____:

On the eve of one of the most important conferences of your life—for you will be confronted with yourself as never before, and with questions pertaining to your personal convictions and Christian faith—I write to reassure you of my confidence and love.

_____ [name], you have been and are a great joy to us. There were early signs of superior ability and leadership. We have observed your growth with pride and thanksgiving.

I need not remind you, of course, that all scholarships and fellowships carry with them a corresponding responsibility. This is uniquely true in your case, since you have to be recommended for it. Therefore, being one of two boys from a student body of more than seven thousand to stand for competitive screening and conference, is in itself a signal recognition.

The other thing I want to say is that whether you receive this coveted fellowship or not, we will think just as much of you, and you must think just as much of yourself. Remember that annually, some of the finest young men in the country are turned down. Everyone cannot win! So condition yourself for either possibility and conduct yourself with high heart regardless of the outcome. Look your best, act your best, think clearly and speak confidently. Your life work will not be determined by this conference, but by what you want to make of yourself.

Inasmuch as this is the year of the Olympic games, I would like to remind you of the motto of the founder of the Olympics and his counsel to all contestants: "The glory is not in the winning but in striving well."

Love,

A MOTHER'S LETTER

Marie Curie, impoverished Polish girl, discoverer of radium, twice recipient of the Nobel Prize, is remembered as one of the greatest of women scientists. Her life was a humble and dedicated epoch from beginning to end. A street accident in Paris claimed the life of her devoted and distinguished husband, Pierre, leaving her with two small children. Years later, after tragedy and triumph, she wrote this New Year's letter to her daughter Irene and her son-in-law, Frederick Joliot-Curie.

December 29, 1928

MY DEAR CHILDREN:

I send you my best wishes for a happy New Year—that is to say, a year of good health, good humor and good work, a year in which you will have pleasure in living every day, without waiting for the days to be gone before finding charm in them, and without putting all hope of pleasure in the days to come. The older one gets the more one feels that the present must be enjoyed; it is a precious gift, comparable to a state of grace.

I am thinking of your little Helene, and forming wishes for her happiness. It is so moving to see the evolution of this little creature who expects everything from you with unlimited confidence, and who certainly believes that you can interpose between her and all suffering. One day she will know that your power does not extend so far—nevertheless one could wish to be able to do that for one's children. At the very least one owes them every effort to give them good health, a peaceful and serene childhood in surroundings of affection, in which their fine confidence will last as long as possible.[3]

TO ONE'S FATHER

William James was in Europe the winter of 1882. Upon arrival in Paris, he received word of his father's illness. He proceeded to

[3] Eve Curie, *Madame Curie, A Biography* (New York: Doubleday, Doran & Company, Inc., 1937), pp. 310–311. Copyright 1937 by Doubleday, Doran & Company, Inc. Used by permission.

London with the intention of securing immediate passage to America, only to discover that his brother Henry had already sailed. With some misgivings, William remained in London, awaiting a message from his family. In such a dilemma, he penned this magnificent letter to his father.

BOLTON ST., LONDON, Dec. 14, 1882

DARLING OLD FATHER:

Two letters, one from my Alice last night, and one from Aunt Kate to Harry just now, have somewhat dispelled the mystery in which the telegrams left your condition; and although their news is several days earlier than the telegrams, I am free to suppose that the latter report only an aggravation of the symptoms the letters describe. It is far more agreeable to think of this than of some dreadful unknown and sudden malady.

We have been so long accustomed to the hypothesis of your being taken away from us, especially during the past ten months, that the thought that this may be your last illness conveys no very sudden shock. You are old enough, you've given your message to the world in many ways and will not be forgotten; you are here left alone, and on the other side, let us hope and pray, dear, dear old Mother is waiting for you to join her. If you go, it will not be an inharmonious thing. Only, if you are still in possession of your normal consciousness, I should like to see you once again before we part. I stayed here only in obedience to the last telegram, and am waiting now for Harry—who knows the exact state of my mind, and who will know yours—to telegraph again what I shall do.

Meanwhile, my blessed old Father, I scribble this line (which may reach you though I should come too late), just to tell you how full of the tenderest memories and feelings about you my heart has for the last few days been filled. In that mysterious gulf of the past into which the present soon will fall and go back and back, yours is still for me the central figure. All my intellectual life I derive from you; and though we have often seemed at odds in the expression thereof, I'm sure there's a harmony somewhere, and that our strivings will combine. What my debt to you is goes beyond all my power of estimating,—so early, so penetrating and so constant has been the influence. You need be in no anxiety about your literary remains. I will see them well taken care of, and that your words shall not suffer for being concealed. At Paris I heard that Milsand, whose name you may remember in the *Revue des Deux Mondes* and elsewhere, was an admirer of the *Secret of Swedenborg*, and Hodgson told me your last book had deeply impressed him. So will it be; especially, I think, if a collection of extracts from your various writings were published, after the manner of the extracts from Carlyle, Ruskin, & Co. I have long thought such a volume would be the best monument to you.—As for us; we shall live on each in his way,—feeling somewhat unprotected, old as we are, for the absence of the parental bosoms as a refuge, but holding fast together in that common sacred memory. We will stand by each other and by Alice, try to transmit the torch in our offspring as you did in us, and when the time comes for being gathered in, I pray we may, if not all, some at least, be as ripe as you. As for myself, I know what trouble I've given you at various times through my peculiarities; and as my own boys grow up, I shall learn more and more of the kind of trial you had to overcome in superintending the development of a creature different from yourself, for whom you felt responsible. I say this merely to show how my sympathy with you is likely to grow much livelier, rather than to fade—and not for the sake of regrets.—As for the other side, and Mother, and our all possibly meeting, I can't say anything. More than ever at this moment do I feel that if that were true, all would be solved and justified. And it comes strangely over me in bidding you good-bye how a life is but a day and expresses mainly but a single note. It is so much like the act of bidding an ordinary good-night. Good-night, my sacred old Father! If I don't see you again—Farewell! a blessed farewell! Your

WILLIAM [4]

TO ONE'S SISTER

Like so many religious workers, John Wesley was disappointed that some members of his family registered so little enthusiasm for his work. One can feel the heaviness of his heart in this letter to Mrs. Martha Hall, his sister.

[4] Henry James, *The Letters of William James* (Boston: Atlantic Monthly Press, 1920), Vol. I, pp. 218–220. Used by permission.

NEAR NEWCASTLE-ON-TYNE
June 14, 1761

DEAR PATTY:

Why should any of us live in the world without doing a little good in it? I am glad you have made a beginning. See that you are not weary in well-doing, for it will often be a cross. But bear the cross; the best fruit grows under the cross.

I have often thought it strange that so few of my relations should be of any use to me in the work of God. My sister Wright was, of whom I should have least expected it; but it was only for a short season. My sister Emily and you, of whom one might have expected more, have, I know not how, kept at a distance, and sometimes cavilled a little, at other times, as it were, approved, but never heartily joined in the work. Where did it stick? Did you not thoroughly understand what my brother and I were doing? Did you not see the truth? Or did the cause lie in your heart? You had no will to join hand in hand. You wanted resolution, spirit, patience. Well, the day is far spent. What you do, do quickly. "Life for delay no time will give."

My work in the country cannot be finished before the latter end of August, as the circuit is now larger by some hundred miles than when I was in the north two years ago. O let the one thing be ever uppermost in our thoughts!

To promote either your temporal or eternal good will always be a pleasure to, Dear Patty,

Your affectionate brother [5]

TO A NIECE

The restless boy who walked the streets of Philadelphia, the lad who rose from a printer's helper to the first and most prominent publisher in the New World, the inventor, the executive, the diplomat, Benjamin Franklin, was also an excellent correspondent. Here is a letter addressed to his niece, Elizabeth Hubbard, on the occasion of the death of a loved one.

[5] George Eayrs, *Letters of John Wesley*, A Selection of Important and New Letters with Introductions and Biographical Notes (London, New York, Toronto: Hodder & Stoughton, Ltd., 1915), pp. 65–66. Used by permission.

PHILADELPHIA, February 22, 1756

DEAR CHILD:

I condole with you, we have lost a most dear and valuable relation, but it is the will of God and Nature that these mortal bodies be laid aside, when the soul is to enter into real life; 'tis rather an embrio state, a preparation for living; a man is not completely born until he be dead; why then should we grieve that a new child is born among the immortals? A new member added to their happy society? We are spirits. That bodies should be lent us, while they can afford us pleasure, assist us in acquiring knowledge, or doing good to our fellow creatures, is a kind of benevolent act of God. When they become unfit for these purposes and afford us pain instead of pleasure—instead of an aid, become an incumbrance and answer none of the intentions for which they were given, it is equally kind and benevolent that a way is provided by which we may get rid of them. Death is that way. We ourselves prudently choose a partial death. In some cases a mangled painful limb, which cannot be restored, we willingly cut off. He who plucks out a tooth, parts with it freely, since the pain goes with it, and he that quits the whole body, parts at once with all pains and possibilities of pains and diseases it was liable to, or capable of making him suffer.

Our friend and we are invited abroad on a party of pleasure—that is to last forever. His chair was first ready and he is gone before us. We could not all conveniently start together, and why should you and I be grieved at this, since we are soon to follow and we know where to find him.

Adieu.

B. FRANKLIN [6]

REMEMBERING ANNIVERSARIES

Anniversaries afford opportunities to reiterate one's love. It is almost unforgivable to overlook an important family date. One may not always be able to find the proper gift, but he can write an appropriate letter.

[6] Leonard W. Labaree and Whitfield J. Bell, Jr., *Mr. Franklin, A Selection from His Personal Letters* (New Haven: Yale University Press, 1956), pp. 268–269. Used by permission.

Samuel Langhorne Clemens (Mark Twain), the gifted American novelist and humorist, was beautifully and permanently in love with his wife, Olivia L. Langdon. Here is one of his birthday greetings.

HARTFORD, November 27, 1875

LIVY DARLING:

Six years have gone by since I made my first great success in life and won you, and thirty years have passed since Providence made preparation for that happy success by sending you into the world. Every day we live together adds to the security of my confidence that we can never any more wish to be separated than that we can ever imagine a regret that we were ever joined. You are dearer to me to-day, my child, than you were upon the last anniversary of this birth-day; you were dearer then than you were a year before—you have grown more and more dear from the first of those anniversaries, and I do not doubt that this precious progression will continue on to the end.

Let us look forward to the coming anniversaries, with their age and their gray hairs without fear and without depression, trusting and believing that the love we bear each other will be sufficient to make them blessed.

So, with abounding affection for you and our babies, I hail this day that brings you the matronly grace and dignity of three decades!

Always yours,
S. L. C.[7]

EXCERPTS FROM STUDENT LETTERS

In one family where there are three children in college, the parents write each child a minimum of five letters a week. Simple arithmetic immediately says that such a program represents fifteen letters a week, sixty a month and five hundred forty for the school year. This is another form of parental discipline and dedication. The mother of these students cannot attend as many parties as some of

[7] Letter "To Mrs. Clemens on Her Thirtieth Birthday" from Mark Twain (Samuel L. Clemens) in Albert Bigelow Paine, *Mark Twain's Letters* (New York and London: Harper & Brothers, 1917), Vol. I, pp. 268–269. Copyright 1917 by Mark Twain Company. Used by permission.

her neighbors, but how could she more profitably employ her time!

The following paragraphs were gleaned from the letters of college students to their parents:

From a Girl

Surprise! I looked in Box _____ [number] . . . and behold a letter! Thanks for writing. It sure makes me feel good to hear from you. I am glad to hear that you are apparently doing fine, but I'm really upset to hear about Daddy. I am glad you insisted that he see a doctor immediately. Daddy is always very sensible about his health, but he sometimes tends to push the little things that bother him out of his mind. Sometimes those little things are warnings of bigger things, so don't let him ignore them.

From a Boy

Thanks for your patience and confidence. You will never know how much it has meant to me during the trying parts of this year and the previous ones. I only hope in my small way I may be able to repay part of it to you.

From a Boy

Whoever said you came to an eastern school to get an education, surely was right! For never have I had to work so hard in all my life. If I ever get out of here (by graduating, that is!) I can at least say they tried to educate me.

From a Boy

All . . . of us . . . are exceedingly thankful for parents of your caliber. Yes, we seldom show it, but we are grateful.

From a Boy

Guess you are the best mother _____ [name of school] ever saw fit to bless. . . .

From a Girl

Before I came up here, I had very shady ideas about religion, or maybe I should say vague. I still don't believe the same things you do, but have developed some new ideas I would like to explain to you. God never seemed very real to me, but now I've found an entirely new God. It's funny, too, that church and chapel talks haven't done it; talking with people and mainly thinking about it in my own mind led me to these conclusions. I just can't wait to tell you about it. It's still not complete, but what is? When you stop growing, Man, you're dead.

SUDDEN SORROW

There are few sorrows comparable to those which envelop a family when one of its members chooses self-destruction. This is particularly tragic when the individual is popular, brilliant, and promising. One of the finest young men of my acquaintance—a versatile and vigorous lad, strong of body, sensitive of spirit, excellent athlete, Phi Beta Kappa—saw fit to end his days just a few weeks before graduating from an outstanding medical school. He was the president of his class, well known and respected on the campus. He was engaged to a charming girl. Apparently the pace was too much and he snapped. During those dark days his equally brilliant and thoughtful brother wrote me this moving letter.

DEAR DR. JONES:

Since you were a friend of my brother _____ [name], I hope you will understand my desire to write and tell you and a few of his other close friends of some of the circumstances which seem to have influenced him to make the decision which he made. It seems only fair to _____'s memory that we who loved him should try to understand the emotional processes, however distorted they were by cumulative physical and mental exhaustion, which impelled him to take his life on the verge of a career which promised so much achievement and satisfaction.

The keynote of _____'s brief life was a passionate giving. Whatever he gave himself to—preparation for a medical practice, the study of music, wrestling on the varsity team at _____ University—he did with ferocious energy. To him life held so many opportunities that he was tantalized, like a child at his first circus, by their wonderful diversity. Whereas most men may hope at most to excel in one field, it was _____'s ambition to master each subject which drew his interest—a truly amazing drive which carried him in his twenty-six years far along the road which to most people spells success.

And yet, because _____ was so aware of the infinity of life's challenges, on the one hand, and of the limitations of man's knowledge on the other—so conscious at every moment of the size of the task which his mind had set for him and which the limitations of his body must betray—he sometimes felt doomed to failure. The exhaustion of overwork naturally aggravated such periods of depression.

To most people, _____'s prospects as he approached graduation from the _____ medical school would have seemed completely fortunate. He was engaged to a fine and charming girl, with whom he had lovingly looked toward the moment of marriage, immediately following his graduation. He stood well up in his class and had won a prized internship at the _____ Hospital. He was popular with his fellow students and was president of the sixty men in his graduating class. He wrote warmly of his affections and his plans to Mother, Dad, and me.

And yet, so exhausting was the effect of his long-sustained exhilaration, so strenuous was his study for his final examinations, so poignant was his realization that his days at _____ were coming to an end and that the prizes for which he had longed were shortly to be his, that at this period _____'s sensitive emotional nature was overtaxed. Undoubtedly an influence was the fact that he had just completed a gruelling service at the hospital, where for weeks he had lived on intimate terms with sorrow and death. To those around him he seemed almost his usual cheerful self, but to one of the members of the family he wrote that his spirits were very low. He was worried about his final examinations, the many details which he had planned so carefully for his wedding, and about his ability to be the ideal physician which he sought to be.

That _____ recognized his oncoming depression is shown by the fact that in these last weeks he consulted the college psychiatrist. To this physician it was evident that _____ was suffering from illness, brought on by overwork. "Many students

have it at some time or other," he said later, "but only one time in
a thousand does it strike one down, as it did _____." _____
was less candid about his condition with us, perhaps because he
had so often heard our entreaties not to overwork and because he
did not want to worry Mother, who was unwell. Thus harassed,
overwrought, unable to sleep, and suffering acutely from his
sinuses and a digestive condition, he reached the breaking point.

The notes which _____ left expressed his love for his fiancée
and his mother and told them that he wanted to save them further worry about him. (It was typical of his illness that he thought
of it as chronic, forgetting the laughter and the self-control which
were normally his.) A truer reflection of the _____ we knew
were the photograph of the fiancée he loved on the desk beside his
goodbye notes, together with a well-thumbed and marked Testament which his minister had given him in 1939, a book of favorite
poems, and medical instruments and papers.

Why did _____ do it? From subsequent conversations
with his roommate, his teachers, and his friends in _____
[city], I could not piece together any fully satisfactory answer.
The dean of the medical school told me _____ was the best ad-
justed man on the campus. Another teacher pointed out that he was
fully in control of his work and had no reason to be fearful. His
fellow students were as puzzled as I. The best explanation which
we could reach was that _____'s death was the result of
physical and mental exhaustion. His act of destruction was merely
the last convulsion in his illness, which until his death had not
been fully recognized.

Now that he has left us I would not want us to deify _____.
He was too human for that. He had his faults as all of us do—
pride, impulsiveness, dogmatism, and occasional intolerance. He
was not a great man, but some who knew him have thought that
he could become a great man. At his best he radiated love and
happiness and joy; he often told me during his four stimulating
years at _____ [school] "Every day's like Christmas,
_____." He liked to help and to inspire, and he dreaded
any hurt to others. "I don't want to make anyone unhappy," he
wrote in his last hour, and in his desperate illness, I doubt that
he could realize the irony of this utterance.

Had _____ died unknown, unloved and unnoticed it would
have meant defeat for him, but it is clear that this is not the
case. The good which he accomplished in his ardent and affirmative young life lives after him in unnumbered hearts.

From people of all ages and conditions expressions of
_____'s help and affection have poured in. I take the liberty of
quoting from one of them which says what I should like to have
said. One of _____'s faculty friends at _____ [name
of school] wrote, "In Burton Parish Churchyard at Williamsburg
there is a sun dial with this inscription: The shadow fell for a moment upon the hour that marked his death; then passed leaving
his name and memory illumined by the eternal sunshine." There
will always be a sunshine around his name and face in my heart.

I hope we remember _____ with a flood of brightest sunshine around him—he who had so much to give and who gave it
so unsparingly.

Sincerely,[8]

LOVE FOR CHRISTMAS

A minister wrote his wife this letter at Christmas. His finances
being depleted by extraordinary expenses, it represented his most
precious gift—love!

DEAR _____:
Before this memorable year fades into history, permit me to
express once more my great and growing love for you. We shall
never experience a more difficult and demanding year. It has been
darkened by sorrow and rainbowed by success. It has been a costly
year. We have paid with our lives—debts, duties, devotions—
that which money could not satisfy. And yet through it all we
have been greatly blessed and gloriously guided.

The church has consumed my every waking moment. It has
been my life. Doubtless I have given _____ [church] too
much of myself and you too little. At any rate, your assistance,
counsel and cooperation when the congregation little dreamed of
your share of the struggle, has been a source of abiding strength.

The home—our home—has gladdened your heart and mine.
Throughout pregnancy, moving, and daily demands, you have
exemplified an enviable stamina and spirit. Our blessed children
and our faith comprise our fortune. Into them we are privileged to
pour our spirit, love and hope.

I have loved you since first I saw you and since first I heard

[8] Used by permission.

the "footsteps of your soul." May God in His boundless mercy
and might, if it be His will, keep us united in love and one in
devotion throughout the coming year.

Always,[9]

"I SHALL BUT LOVE THEE BETTER"

In her *Sonnets from the Portuguese,* Elizabeth Barrett Browning
reached ethereal heights of expression. Having overcome all fears,
the poet crowned her declaration of love with this sweeping envelop-
ment of life and faith.

> How do I love thee? Let me count the ways.
> I love thee to the depth and breadth and height
> My soul can reach, when feeling out of sight
> For the ends of Being and Ideal Grace.
> I love thee to the level of every day's
> Most quiet need, by sun and candle-light.
> I love thee freely, as men strive for Right;
> I love thee purely, as they turn from Praise.
> I love thee with the passion put to use
> In my old griefs, and with my childhood's faith.
> I love thee with a love I seemed to lose
> With my lost saints,—I love thee with the breath,
> Smiles, tears, of all my life!—and, if God choose,
> I shall but love thee better after death.

This is the language and lift of love!

[9] Used by permission.

Appendix

CLASSIFICATIONS OF MAIL

First Class

First-class mail includes letters, postal and post cards, air mail (not exceeding 8 ounces) sealed and unsealed, matters wholly or partly in writing (except authorized additions to those relegated to lower or slower postal services) and matters sealed or closed against inspection.

FIRST CLASS [1]

RATES

Kind of Mail	Rate
All first-class mail except postal and post cards and drop letters	4¢ per ounce
Drop letters	3¢ per ounce
Single postal cards and post cards	3¢ each
Double postal cards and post cards	6¢ (3¢ each portion)
(reply portion of double post card does not have to bear postage when originally mailed).	
Business reply mail (see 131.23):	
Cards	5¢ each
Other than cards:	
Weight not over 2 ounces	4¢ per ounce plus 2¢ per piece
Weight over 2 ounces	4¢ per ounce plus 5¢ per piece

[1] *Domestic Postage Rates and Fees, Postal Manual, POD Publication 3,* January 1959 (U.S. Government Printing Office), p. 3. Used by permission.

Second Class [2]

One must qualify to use second-class postal privileges. Moreover, it imposes certain responsibilities on the sender.

Publishers and senders must determine the number of issues that will appear annually and also establish a frequency schedule —daily, weekly, monthly, quarterly, semiweekly, biweekly, semimonthly, or whatever frequency desired. This type of mailing is often used by the church and other nonprofit organizations, and should be carefully understood and correlated with suggestions from the local post office.

	January 1, 1961 Cents per pound or fraction thereof *
Nonadvertising portion	2.5
Advertising portion:	
First and second zones	3.0
Third zone	4.0
Fourth zone	6.0
Fifth zone	8.0
Sixth zone	10.0
Seventh zone	12.0
Eighth zone	14.0

* Minimum ½¢ per copy.

Applications for Second-Class Privileges

Applications for Publications and News Agents that do not have Second-Class Privileges.

An application must be filed by the publisher before a publication may be mailed at the second-class rates. Two copies of the issue described in the application must also be filed. If the publication is printed in a foreign language, a brief translation of the contents of the copies must be furnished. A synopsis of each article and advertisement is usually sufficient. News agents must file applications before they may mail second-class publications at the second-class rates. Copies of all applica-

[2] *Ibid.*, p. 4.

tion forms may be obtained from local postmasters. The headings on the forms describe what information must be furnished by publishers and news agents. Use the following forms:

a. File application Form 3501 for second-class privileges for a publication that meets the basic qualifications at the post office of the place where the known place of publication is located.

b. File application Form 3502 for second-class mail privileges for a publication of an institution or society that does not meet the basic qualifications at the post office of the place where the known place of publication is located.

c. File application Form 3501-A for permission to mail foreign publications in the United States at the post office at which the copies are to be mailed.

d. File application Form 3501-A for registry of a person or firm as news agent with the privilege of mailing second-class publications at the post office where mailings are to be made.[3]

Applications for Publications That Have Second-Class Privileges

After a publication has obtained second-class mail privileges, applications may be filed for the following additional privileges:

a. Publishers of newspapers or periodicals of non-profit religious, educational, scientific, philanthropic, agricultural, labor, veterans', or fraternal organizations or associations may file applications by letter to the postmaster for the special rate. See 132.122, *Postal Manual*. They must submit evidence to establish their non-profit status and to show that they come within one of the categories stated.[4]

Quite obviously, the rates of second-class mail vary, depending on the places of origin and destination. If mailed in the county of publication, it is one price; outside, another. Weight and destination are always factors.

Third Class

Mailers of third-class mail at other than bulk rates may use any method of paying postage, and may mail any number of pieces at one time, except when permit imprints are used.[5]

[3] *Mailing Permits, Postal Manual, POD Publication 13,* June 1960 (U.S. Government Printing Office), pp. 6–7.
[4] *Ibid.*
[5] *Ibid.,* p. 8.

Third-Class Mailings

Mailing Statement. Complete and submit with each mailing: a. Mailing Statement, POD Form 3602, for mail with permit imprints, or b. Mailing Statement, POD Form 3602-PC, for mail bearing precanceled stamps or meter stamps.

Preparation of Mailing. Sort, face, and tie bulk mail into packages both lengthwise and crosswise with twine strong enough to withstand handling in the mails (a breaking point of 10 pounds or more will qualify). Labels should be large enough to cover the address on the exposed piece of mail and to keep the label from sliding out from under the twine. Prepare packages as follows:

a. Direct Package. When there are 10 or more pieces for any one post office (or station or branch if its name forms a part of the address), face all addresses one way except the last which must be reversed to expose its address on the outside of the package. Do not label direct packages.

b. State Package. After direct-package pieces are removed, if there are 10 or more pieces remaining for any one State, face all addresses one way and tie the pieces into a package. Cover the top address with a label bearing the name of the State.

c. Mixed Packages. If there are less than 10 pieces per State (for instance, 6 for Delaware, 8 for Maryland, 5 for Virginia), face all addresses one way and tie the pieces into a package. Cover the top address with a label bearing the words *Mixed States*.[6]

Fourth Class

Should you desire to crate or ship any of your members, you would doubtless use a fourth-class mailing, since it covers "live animals and all other matter, not included in the first, second or third-class," though I am advised "only certain live animals are mailable."

Mixed Mailings

This applies when mail of higher class is included with mail of lower classes or a combination of two classes.

---

[6] *How to Prepare Second and Third Class Mailings, Postal Manual, POD Publication 21*, November 1957, p. 10.

Combination Mailings of Two Classes

Letters attached to Other Mail. A letter or other mail of the first class may be placed in an envelope carrying postage at the first-class rate, or airmail rate in case of air parcels, and tied or otherwise securely attached to the address side of a parcel or package. The envelope must be addressed the same as the parcel. Combination envelopes or containers having separate portions for a letter and mail of another class may be used for mailing together two classes of mail.

Postage. Postage on a parcel of second-, third-, or fourth-class mail must be prepaid at the appropriate rate for the class involved and placed in the upper right corner of the address space. Postage for the letter must be attached to the envelope or portion of container in which the letter is enclosed. If mailed by air, postage at the airmail rate must be paid for the letter.

Markings Required. If a letter is a printed circular prepaid at the third-class rate, the envelope must be left unsealed and endorsed *Third Class*. Envelopes, containing first-class mail attached to parcels of other classes may be marked *First Class* or *Letter Enclosed*. In every case the address and return card should appear on the envelopes or containers having separate portions for a letter and mail of another class. The address of the letter may be considered as the address of the whole piece.[7]

Postage Meters

To use this time-saving and businesslike device for stamping mail, one must make application for a meter license. (Use Form 3601.) Once a license is obtained it may be revoked for improper use, or for allowing the machine to be idle for twelve consecutive months.

Airmail

Description

Airmail is mail carried by air and by the fastest connecting surface carriers and given the most expeditious handling in dispatch and delivery. Airmail is not given special delivery to the addressee unless a special delivery fee is paid in addition to the airmail postage.

[7] *Combination Mailing, Postal Manual, POD Publication 14*, October 1956, p. 2.

Articles Acceptable

Mail of all classes, except that which may be damaged by low temperatures or high altitudes, is accepted for airmail.[8]

Registered Mail

What May Be Registered:
a. First-class mail
b. Airmail not likely to damage from freezing
c. Second-class mail
d. Third-class mail
e. Fourth-class mail prepaid with postage at the first-class rate
f. Business reply cards and envelopes if you pay only the registration fee.[9]

Registered mail is the safest of all mail. It not only assures the sender of hand to hand handling, but also the recipient must sign a delivery slip. Virtually any class of mail may be registered. There are additional fees of course. This type of mail is especially recommended for transmitting valuable documents and legal notices.

Insurance

Purpose. You may obtain payment for loss of, rifling of, or damage to domestic mail by having it insured.

Classes of Mail to Which Applicable. You may insure only third-and fourth-class mail or airmail which contains third-or fourth-class matter. Insured airmail may contain incidental first-class enclosures. The mail must bear the complete names and addresses of sender and addressee. The following are not acceptable for insurance:
a. Parcels containing matter offered for sale, addressed to prospective purchasers who have not ordered or authorized their sending. If such matter is received in the mails, payment will not be made for loss, rifling, or damage.
b. Nonmailable matter.
c. Articles that are so fragile as to prevent their safe carriage in the mails regardless of packaging.

[8] *Domestic Postage Rates and Fees, Postal Manual, POD Publication 3,* January 1959, p. 18.
[9] *Ibid.,* p. 19.

d. Articles which are not adequately packed to withstand normal handling in the mails.[10]

Special Delivery

Description of Special Delivery

Points of Delivery. Special-delivery mail is given immediate delivery at the office of address during prescribed hours to:
  a. Points within a radius of 1 mile of any post office, station or branch.
  b. Points within the delivery limits of any post office having letter carrier service.
  c. Points within one-half mile of a rural route, if there is a passable road leading to the addressee's dwelling or place of business.

Transporting and Delivering. Special-delivery mail is handled and transported in the same manner and with the same expedition as first-class mail. Payment of a special-delivery fee does not insure safety of delivery or provide for the payment of indemnity. Money or other valuables sent special delivery should also be registered. Insured and COD mail may be sent special delivery.[11]

Special Handling

Description of Special Handling

Special-handling service is available for fourth-class mail only, including that which is insured or sent COD. It provides the most expeditious handling, dispatch and transportation available, but does not provide for special delivery. Special-handling parcels are delivered as parcel post is ordinarily delivered, on regular scheduled trips. The special-handling fee (or special-delivery fee) must be paid on all parcels that must be given special attention in handling, transportation, and delivery, such as parcels containing baby chicks or other baby poultry, package bees carried outside mail bags, baby alligators, etc.[12]

Certified Mail

Certified mail service provides for a receipt to the sender and a record of delivery at the office of address. No record is kept at the office at

[10] *Ibid.*, p. 20.
[11] *Ibid.*, p. 22.
[12] *Ibid.*, p. 23.

which mailed. It is handled in the ordinary mails and no insurance coverage is provided.[13]

The mail is endorsed with the words "CERTIFIED MAIL," and a number appears thereon.

These statements describe a wide variety of mailings, all of which are used at one time or another by the church. Your Post Office will be glad to send you literature on any problem and answer specific queries.

[13] *Ibid.*

Index

211